School Counseling
TO CLOSE THE
Achievement Gap

School Counseling

TO CLOSE THE

Achievement Gap

A
SOCIAL JUSTICE
Framework for Success

Cheryl Holcomb-McCoy

CORWIN PRESS
A SAGE Publications Company
Thousand Oaks, CA 91320

For information:

Corwin Press
A Sage Publications Company
2455 Teller Road
Thousand Oaks, California 91320
www.corwinpress.com

Sage Publications Ltd.
1 Oliver's Yard
55 City Road
London EC1Y 1SP
United Kingdom

Sage Publications India Pvt. Ltd.
B 1/I 1 Mohan Cooperative
  Industrial Area
Mathura Road, New Delhi 110 044
India

Sage Publications Asia-Pacific Pte. Ltd.
33 Pekin Street #02-01
Far East Square
Singapore 048763

Printed in the United States of America.

Library of Congress Cataloging-in-Publication Data

Holcomb-McCoy, Cheryl.
School counseling to close the achievement gap : a social justice
framework for success/Cheryl Holcomb-McCoy.
    p. cm.
Includes bibliographical references and index.
ISBN-13: 978-1-4129-4183-9 (cloth)
ISBN-13: 978-1-4129-4184-6 (pbk.)
    1. Educational counseling—United States. 2. Student counselors—In-service
training—United States. 3. Academic achievement—United states. I. Title.

LB1027.5.H635 2007
371.4—dc22

2006102665

This book is printed on acid-free paper.

07   08   09   10   11   10   9   8   7   6   5   4   3   2   1

Acquisitions Editor:	Stacy Wagner
Editorial Assistant:	Joanna Coelho
Production Editor:	Veronica Stapleton
Copy Editor:	Edward Meidenbauer
Typesetter:	C&M Digitals (P) Ltd.
Proofreader:	Joyce Li
Indexer:	Rick Hurd
Cover Designer:	Rose Storey
Graphic Designer:	Lisa Miller

Contents

Preface

The concept of this book began when I was an elementary school counselor in the Washington, DC, area. Like most counselors, I saw and heard everything. I heard parents' stories about insensitive and biased teachers, I heard teachers' stories about negligent and "unfit" parents, and I heard administrators' stories about unrealistic district policies and goals. I learned that everyone has a story in a school. But most important, I learned that counselors are in the optimum position to bring those stories together and create change for students.

My first year in teaching changed the way in which I viewed education, particularly education of low-income and ethnic minority students (or students-of-color). As a beginning teacher and later as a beginning counselor, I believed the myth that if students didn't succeed in school, it was because of their unwillingness to achieve. However, as I became more experienced I learned that it is not that simple. In many cases, schools fail students by implementing biased policies and tolerating culturally incompetent educators. I also learned that it is often ethnic minority students who receive covert and sometimes overt messages from educators that they are not valued and "smart enough" to be successful. My peers, who included White teachers and teachers-of-color, were both guilty of this "lack of faith" in all students.

My disappointment in schools and school counselors led me to write this book. Although there are many well-intentioned and truly caring school counselors who make an impact on the lives of students, there are far too many school counselors who are silent and keepers of the status quo. It is time for school counselors to become more visible in education debates and to make cutting-edge decisions about the future of schools and education. With school counselors' training in counseling, education, group dynamics, human development, and systems theory, they have the unique capacity to understand students' academic as well as social and emotional development. If any group of educators can make a difference in the lives of students, it's school counselors.

While writing this book, I thought about my own personal journey as a mother of two African American children. The constant struggle to manage teachers' and other peoples' negative perceptions of not only my children but all African American children is overwhelming and anxiety-provoking. More important, I worry about my children and the mixed messages that they receive about their worthiness and abilities. My hope is that they will be able to endure and thrive in a world that does not always value them and find them capable. Writing this book has been therapeutic, and I am hopeful that school counselors will understand how their work can help parents like me rest better and feel confident that there is one person in our students' schools who understands our story.

PURPOSE

The purpose of *School Counseling to Close the Achievement Gap: A Social Justice Approach* is to introduce school counselors to six key elements of school counseling that can help to close the achievement gap and remedy issues of inequities in schools. For many years, school counselors have been blamed for biased advising, faulty assumptions, and discriminating practices that bar groups of students from opportunities in schools. In many cases, this blaming is justified. There are many school counselors who are guilty of damaging the lives of students. Although I believe that most counselors unintentionally promote inequities, I do believe there is a benefit to maintaining the status quo. With the status quo comes familiarity and no need to relearn or reeducate oneself. I am hopeful that after reading this book, that school counselors will feel energized to make changes in their approach to working with students and to take a stand against oppressive practices and the status quo.

I would like to mention that even though a large part of this book is focused on the oppression experienced by students-of-color, the concepts can certainly be applied to any oppressed group of students. I believe that once counselors understand equity and social justice, they will begin to see inequities everywhere and across many diverse groups.

Acknowledgments

Writing a book on the achievement gap was an emotional experience because it deals with a topic that I feel extremely passionate about. The support of colleagues, students, friends, and family, however, gave me the will to complete it. Most of all, however, I would like to thank my family for all of their support and encouragement. My children, Niles and Nia, are my inspiration for writing the book, for they represent the many children who are affected each day by the inequitable practices occurring in schools. Because of my love for them, and all children, I wrote this book. I also want to thank my husband, Alvin, for his love and faith in my ability to convey a message that others would want to hear. I love you Al. And most important, I want to thank my parents who have been my inspiration and role models for what it means to be a passionate educator. Thanks Mom and Dad (Colethia and Frederick Holcomb), for your many years of support, guidance, and love. I love you both!

Corwin Press would like to thank the following peer reviewers for their editorial insight and guidance:

Maryann Baldwin
Chamberlain Advanced Placement Scholars (CAPS) Guidance Counselor
AP Coordinator
Chamberlain High School
Tampa, Florida

Judy Bowers
Supervisor of Guidance and Counseling
Tucson Unified School District
Tucson, Arizona

Stuart F. Chen-Hayes
Associate Professor, Counselor Education and School Counseling
Lehman College of the City University of New York
Bronx, New York

Sharon Johnson
Doctor, Professor Emeritus
Walden University
Educational Consulting
Retired from California State University, Los Angeles
San Juan Capistrano, California

Gloria L. Kumagi
Coordinator, Licensure and Leadership Development
Educational Policy and Administration
University of Minnesota
Minneapolis, Minnesota

James L. Moore, III
Associate Professor in Counselor Education
The Ohio State University
Columbus, Ohio

Christopher Sink
Professor and Chair, School Counseling
School of Education
Seattle Pacific University
Seattle, Washington

Jennifer White-Peters
School Counselor
Burlington City Junior School
Burlington, New Jersey

About the Author

 **Cheryl Holcomb-McCoy** received her PhD in counseling and educational development from the University of North Carolina at Greensboro (UNCG). She is an Associate Professor in the Department of Counseling and Personnel Services at the University of Maryland, College Park. Her areas of research specialization include multicultural school counseling, school counselor multicultural self-efficacy, and urban school counselor preparation. She has written numerous book chapters and refereed articles on issues pertaining to diversity in school counselor education. Dr. Holcomb-McCoy is a former elementary school counselor and kindergarten teacher.

In 2000, Dr. Holcomb-McCoy was elected National Secretary of Chi Sigma Iota International and was the recipient of the Chi Sigma Iota Outstanding Research Award in 1998. She was named Maryland Counselor Educator of the Year in 2001 and was awarded the Exemplary Diversity Leadership Award by the Association for Multicultural Counseling and Development (AMCD) in 2007. Dr. Holcomb-McCoy has served on the editorial boards of the *Professional School Counseling Journal, Journal of Counseling and Development, Counselor Education and Supervision Journal,* and the *Journal of Multicultural Counseling and Development.* She is currently serving as the American School Counselor Association Diversity Professional Network Chairperson and is a consultant for the College Board's National Office of School Counselor Advocacy. She resides with her husband and two children in Potomac, Maryland.

1

The Achievement Gap

Our Ultimate Challenge

C arlos, a fifth-grade Latino student in an urban school district, wrote the following essay:

> When I grow up I will get married and have two kids and I will make lots of money. I will be a good dad because I will play with my kids and bring money home to pay for all the food and bills. I will treat my wife nice and not fight with her about money. I am going to work at an office building and be the manager. Not like the men I see on the corner. I am going to have beautiful cars and a nice life.

At Carlos's elementary school, only 8% of his classmates meet fifth-grade reading standards on the state assessment. Just 10% of them met state mathematics standards, 4% met writing standards, and 3% met state science standards. Last year, the graduation rate at Carlos's neighborhood high school was 48% and if Carlos is one of those 48% who graduate, chances are that he will not have the skills necessary to pursue further education successfully, much less manage a business. His future income will most likely be far less than he needs for the "nice life" he envisions. Unfortunately, Carlos's chances of realizing his dreams are not good. For a snapshot of high school dropout rates by gender and race, see Table 1.1 below.

Another fifth-grade student, Jacob, attends an elementary school 25 miles from Carlos's school in a more affluent White suburban neighborhood. His aspirations are similar to the ones Carlos wrote about. Jacob's chances for realizing his dreams, however, are not as slim. At Jacob's school, 97% of the fifth-grade class met reading standards and 96% met math standards. Eleventh-grade students in Jacob's neighborhood high school had an average ACT score of 24.3; 87% of the students met state standards in reading, 89% in mathematics, 84% in writing, and 89% in science. The graduation rate was 98% last year. By attending these schools, Jacob will be well on his way to having a "nice life."

As Carlos graduates from fifth grade and prepares for his future, the next 6 years of his schooling represent a journey of roadblocks and the challenge of being successful in a system set up for "other people." In contrast, Jacob's next 6 years are a bridge to attaining his dreams and successful experiences with people and systems that believe in his abilities. That is not to say that Carlos will not succeed, but he will have to have fortitude, resolve, and a great amount of support, faith, and good fortune. He will certainly need better schooling and more opportunities in school than he has now. Without additional intervention from the educational system, educators, and community, Carlos is far more likely to end up like one of those men he "sees on the corner."

Table 1.1 Percentage of high school dropouts (status dropouts) among persons 16–24 years old by gender and race: 2000–2004.

Year	Total			Male			Female		
	White	Black	Hispanic	White	Black	Hispanic	White	Black	Hispanic
2000	6.9	13.1	27.8	7.0	15.3	31.8	6.9	11.1	23.5
2001	7.3	10.9	27.0	7.9	13.0	31.6	6.7	9.0	22.1
2002	6.5	11.3	25.7	6.7	12.8	29.6	6.3	9.9	21.2
2003	6.3	10.9	23.5	7.1	12.5	26.7	5.6	9.5	20.1
2004	6.8	11.8	23.8	7.1	13.5	28.5	6.4	10.2	18.5

NOTE: "Status dropouts" are 16- to 24-year-olds who are not enrolled in school and who have not completed a high school program regardless of when they left school. People who have received GED credentials are counted as high school completers. From the U.S. Department of Commerce, Census Bureau, Current Population Survey. Copyright 2004.

The disparities between Carlos's and Jacob's stories are all too familiar and can be echoed across the United States. Carlos's and Jacob's futures represent what we think of when we hear the term *achievement gap*. The term describes the extreme disparities between children who live in low-income, impoverished communities and children who live in affluent, middle-to-high income communities. This moral and educational problem is something educators have sought to solve, but the gap persists and remains an ongoing issue.

SCHOOL COUNSELING AND THE GAP

Most school counselors would say that they are doing all that they can do to help students like Carlos. Rightly so, most school counselors are concerned about the achievement gap and believe that they are doing everything they can to close the gap. One missing link, however, is that many school counselors are not trained to assist students to overcome societal, familial, and educational barriers. In most cases, school counselors will know how to invite Carlos's parents to participate in school events, how to work with Carlos in a small counseling group, how to counsel Carlos about friendship issues, and how to consult with his teachers about his low grades. However, school counselors are rarely prepared to challenge Carlos's teachers regarding what may be their low expectations of Latino male students or to advocate for more educational support sources in Carlos's community. These are the types of activities that are needed to help Carlos persevere and overcome obstacles to achieving his dreams. As a professional counselor and counselor educator with extensive background in multicultural training, I believe that these are the types of activities that should be in school counselor job descriptions. This book is my attempt to offer to school counselors the lessons and strategies that research and experience have shown will ensure students like Carlos have opportunities to succeed.

WHERE WE HAVE BEEN AND
WHERE WE ARE HEADED

For many years, school counselors or guidance counselors have, in part, been blamed for the perpetuation of educational inequalities in schools by supporting tracking systems and by denying students the opportunity to enter or remain in advanced tracks. Although every school has its educators who prefer the status quo, there are many wonderful counselors who help students achieve their dreams. But there is still much more that school counselors can do to help all students (particularly poor and ethnic minority students) achieve. The American School Counselor Association (ASCA) has begun to address this challenge by posing the question, "How are students different because of what school counselors do?" As a result of this question, ASCA created its National Model, a framework for school counseling programs. See the diagram in Figure 1.1 below.

The ASCA National Model's focus is on bridging counseling and academic achievement via systemic and collaborative efforts between counselors, teachers, administrators, parents, and students. More important, the National Model emphasizes accountability and the use of results reports, school counselor performance standards, and program audits. Also, included in the National Model are National Standards that act as the objectives for student outcomes. These student outcomes are divided into three areas: *academic*

Figure 1.1 ASCA National Model Diagram

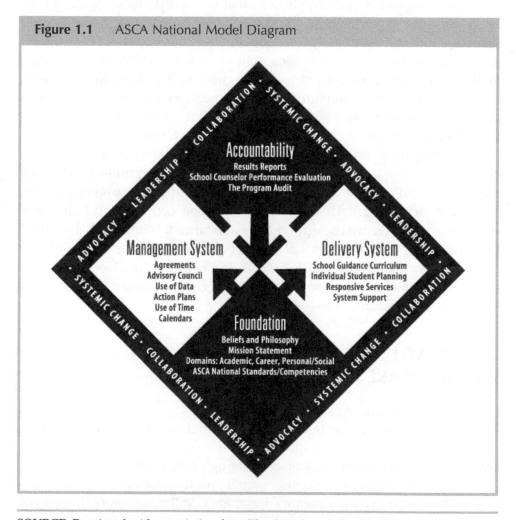

SOURCE: Reprinted with permission from The American School Counselor Association.

development, career development, and *personal and social development.* The ASCA National Model and Standards have clearly moved the school counseling profession in a direction in which counselors act as an integral part of the school's mission and are linked to the academic focus of today's schools.

However, even if counselors design their programs aligned with the Model, there will still be children like Carlos who will not be served or who need additional barriers removed before they can achieve. This is where this book will help. What else do counselors need to do *beyond* the ASCA model to help all students achieve?

THE POWER OF SCHOOL COUNSELORS

School counselors must assume the power that they have in schools, power that enables them to either dampen the dreams of students or help them to realize their dreams. As evidence, I have heard the following statements from adults:

- "My counselor said that I would never get into college . . . that's why I never applied. I wish I hadn't listened to her."
- "My counselor really believed in my ability. If it hadn't been for him telling me that I was capable, I probably would have ended up like my friends—hanging out and getting into trouble."

These statements are evidence that school counselors have an enormous amount of power that, if channeled in the right direction, would help close the gap. Of course, counselors are not the only people in a school building who make important decisions about students. However, the school counselor can be the one person in a school that will act as an advocate for students. This book will propose ways in which school counselors can make a difference in the lives of all children.

ACHIEVEMENT GAP DEFINED

As mentioned previously, one of the major problems facing the educational system in the United States is the widespread inequity in educational achievement and opportunity across ethnic and socioeconomic groups. On a variety of measures, such as high school completion and college participation rates, Advanced Placement course enrollment, and standardized achievement tests, ethnically diverse (with the exception of Asian Americans) and low-income students have much lower levels of achievement. This gap has become more widely known as the *achievement gap* and denotes when groups of students with relatively equal ability don't achieve in school at the same levels. In fact, one group often far exceeds the achievement level of the other. There are gaps between girls and boys, gaps between poor and wealthy students, and gaps between urban and suburban students, just to name a few. But the most glaring gap, nationally and locally, is among races. Even when parents' income and wealth is comparable, African Americans, Native Americans, Latinos, and immigrants for whom English is not a first language lag behind English-speaking, native-born, White students. The evidence for these gaps has been documented repeatedly (Chubb & Loveless, 2001; Education Trust, 2006; Fine, 2001; Haycock, Jerald, & Huang, 2001).

Why focus on the achievement gap at all? One reason for widespread concern over the gap in student achievement is that it involves substantial social and economic costs. Low educational achievement is associated with high unemployment, lower earnings, higher crime, and a greater dependency on welfare and other social services. The social costs of these outcomes can be staggering. Another reason for the widespread concern over the achievement gap is that the ethnic diversity of the U.S. population is increasingly growing and, by 2020, it is expected that school districts in major cities will have student populations consisting of predominately students-of-color (Henig, Hula, Orr, & Pedescleaux, 1999).

The achievement gap is a complex problem and parallels other societal gaps (such as poverty) that differ among ethnic and socioeconomic groups. Although it is impossible to discuss the achievement gap without discussing these other societal gaps, the achievement gap seems to be most prevalent in those schools that are not attending to issues of social justice; that is, to issues of equity, equality, and possibility for all students. Social justice champions the belief that one can change the world and that all persons may contribute to the whole of society while striving for their own potential. Acquiring an awareness and acknowledgment of social justice is a logical goal in closing the achievement gap. That is the focus of this book.

A CLOSER LOOK AT THE GAP

Although schools may have little influence over poverty or community factors, what goes on in schools could lessen their negative effect. For decades, policymakers, researchers, and school reformers have sought ways in which schools could address the achievement gap. Strategies have focused on school funding, teacher quality, student interventions and motivation, school organization, management, school climate, market competition, and school accountability to the public. The following pages offer a look at where the gaps and inequities exist.

Standardized Tests

Student achievement gaps among ethnic and socioeconomic groups are large and persistent. Despite long-term progress by African American and Latino and Latina students, the gaps on various standardized tests remain wide. For instance, on the 2004 reading trends test of the National Assessment of Educational Progress (NAEP), the average score of African American students at age 17 was slightly lower than the White students at age 13. In math, the average score for African American 13-year-olds was more than 20 points below that of White 13-year-olds—roughly the equivalent of two grade levels behind. In science, the average score for Latino 9-year-olds was the equivalent of more than three grade levels behind that of White 9-year-olds.

According to NAEP, in the 18- to 24-year-old group, about 90% of Whites and 94% of Asian Americans had either completed high school or earned a GED (National Assessment of Educational Progress, 2004). Among African Americans, the rate dropped to 81% and among Latinos to 63%. And, approximately 76% of White high school graduates and 86% of Asian American high school graduates went directly to college, compared with 71% of African American and 71% of Latino graduates (Green & Forster, 2003). For those who stay in high school to graduate, low-income and ethnic minority students have more limited access to the rigorous coursework needed for college readiness.

Course-Taking Patterns

Disparities exist in students' course-taking patterns as well. Data from the U.S. Department of Education indicate that approximately 62% of White, African American, and Hispanic or Latino high school graduates each were enrolled in an Algebra 1 course in high school in 1998. But that pattern did not hold for higher-level math courses. Whereas 64% of White students took Algebra 2, only 55% of African American and 48% of Hispanic or Latino students were also enrolled. Even larger gaps appear in honors course enrollment: 7.5% of White students, 3.4% of African American students, and 3.7% of Hispanic or Latino students took Advanced Placement calculus (U.S. Department of Education, 2000).

The news is not all bad. Today, there are more African American and Latino students taking academically rigorous courses than in the past. But researchers have found that schools in culturally and linguistically diverse or high-poverty areas often offer a less-rigorous curriculum to begin with. Because they cover less material or give less homework they fail to challenge students. This is a problem because research has found that students enrolled in challenging courses—in topics such as algebra, trigonometry, chemistry, and advanced English—usually have higher standardized test scores than their peers.

Teacher Experience and Expectations

Low-income students and students-of-color are more likely to be taught by less-experienced teachers than are White students. Researchers have cited this factor as one of the most critical variables for explaining the achievement gap. There is a correlation between higher teacher certification scores and higher student achievement scores. Teachers in districts where there are high percentages of Black or Latino students tend to have lower scores on their certification tests.

Studies have suggested that teachers sometimes have lower academic expectations for African American and Latino children than they do for Whites or Asian American. By setting low expectations, teachers run the risk of perpetuating the achievement gap because they do not encourage African American and Latino students to follow a rigorous curriculum.

Cultural Competence

Educators' lack of cultural competence or lack of cultural sensitivity can negatively impact the achievement of students. Educators who lack the cultural knowledge, awareness, and skills to work with diverse groups of students and parents are less equipped to nurture the academic achievement of diverse students.

Availability of Resources

Resource disparities handicap schools. Low-minority schools tend to be much better funded and have all-around stronger resources than do high-minority schools. The same relationship holds true for schools in low-poverty versus high-poverty areas. There is persuasive evidence that this factor contributes to the achievement gap. For example, data from the NAEP show the achievement gap between low-poverty and high-poverty schools increased throughout the 1990s (Education Trust, 2001).

Special Education

Another critical gap in student achievement is the gap in the identification of special education students. Students-of-color, specifically Native American and African American students, are significantly more likely than White students to be identified as having a disability. For example, in most states, African American students are identified at 1.5 to 4 times the rate of White students in the disability categories of mental retardation and emotional disturbance (The Civil Rights Project, 2003). In addition, Latino and Asian American students are underidentified in cognitive disability categories compared with White students, raising questions about whether the special education needs of these children are being met (Losen & Orfield, 2002). Once identified, most students-of-color are significantly more likely to be removed from the general education program and educated in a more restrictive environment.

Losen and Orfield report even more disturbing statistics:

• Among high school youth with disabilities, about 75% of African American students, as compared with 47% of White students, are not employed two years out of school. Three to five years out of school, the arrest rate for African Americans with disabilities is 40%, as compared with 27% for Whites.

• The identification of African American students for mental retardation is pronounced in the South. Southern states constituted nearly three quarters of the states with unusually high incidence levels, where between 2.75 and 5.41% of the African Americans enrolled were labeled as mentally retarded. The prevalence of mental retardation for Whites nationally was approximately .75% in 2001, and in no state did the incidence of mental retardation among Whites rise above 2.32%.

• Poverty does not explain the gross racial disparities in mental retardation and emotional disturbance, nor does it explain disparities in the category of specific learning disability or any medically diagnosed disabilities.

Thinking About . . . Students With Special Needs

What is the process of identifying students for special education at your school? Are there a disproportionate number of students-of-color in special education programs? If so, has your staff discussed what to do about it?

College Education

When looking at college graduation statistics, young African Americans are only about half as likely as White students to earn a bachelor's degree by age 29 and young Latinos are only one-third as likely as Whites to earn a college degree (Haycock, 2001). Although the number of African American, Latino, and Native American students enrolled in college has risen, those enrollment figures are far below the representation of those students in K–12 schools and below what would be projected for average college attendance given those K–12 enrollment figures (Allen, 2003).

Another way to illustrate the achievement gap is to examine SAT college entrance examination scores. A review of 2006 SAT scores revealed that African American students performed 93 points lower on the critical reading section and 107 points lower in mathematics. Asian American students, however, scored 42 points higher than White students in mathematics and 149 points higher than African American students (see Figures 1.2 and 1.3).

The Gap Across the Educational Continuum

Although the achievement gap is typically seen as a problem affecting school-age children, in fact the gap first opens during the preschool years. Studies consistently show that poor and ethnically diverse children have already fallen behind well before they enter kindergarten. These children, as young as 3 years old, already perform far below average on tests of school readiness. Unless one believes that this poor performance is due entirely or

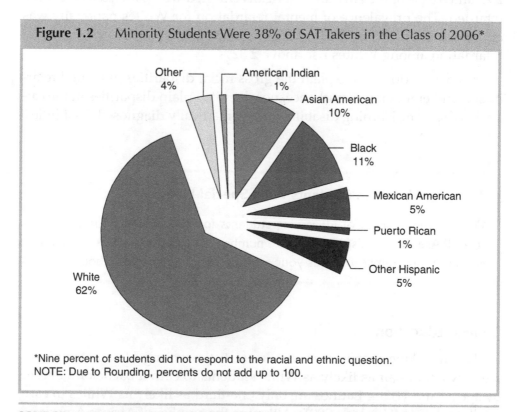

Figure 1.2   Minority Students Were 38% of SAT Takers in the Class of 2006*

Other
4%

American Indian
1%

Asian American
10%

Black
11%

Mexican American
5%

Puerto Rican
1%

Other Hispanic
5%

White
62%

*Nine percent of students did not respond to the racial and ethnic question.
NOTE: Due to Rounding, percents do not add up to 100.

SOURCE: "2006 College-Bound Seniors" Copyright © 2006 The College Board, www.college board.com. Reproduced with permission.

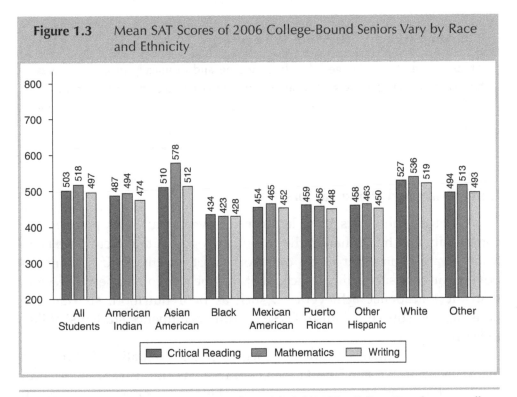

Figure 1.3 Mean SAT Scores of 2006 College-Bound Seniors Vary by Race and Ethnicity

SOURCE: "2006 College-Bound Seniors" Copyright© 2006 The College Board, www.college board.com. Reproduced with permission.

primarily to genetic factors, it follows that the preschool environments of poor and ethnically diverse children are deficient in supplying the types of experiences that promote school readiness (Haskins & Rouse, 2005).

Data from the U.S. Department of Education (2006) indicate that some groups of young children have higher rates of participation in center-based preschool programs than others. For example, in each of the years observed, a greater percentage of middle-to-high income children aged 3–5 participated in center-based programs than low-income children. The difference in rates of participation between children from low-income and middle-income families was 13% in 2005 (47% vs. 60%).

In addition, a greater percentage of African American and White children than Hispanic or Latino children participate in center-based preschool programs. In 2005, 66% of African American children and 59% of White children participated in such programs, compared with 43% of Hispanic or Latino children. White and Latino middle-income children were more likely than their low-income peers to participate in center-based preschool programs, whereas no measurable difference was found between low-income and middle-income African American children.

> **Thinking About . . . Barriers to Learning**
>
> Think about the challenges that low-income and ethnically diverse families face on a regular basis (e.g., discrimination, child care tuition, economic strain, limited access to resources, etc.). How do these challenges affect the education of children?

Community and Home Factors

Although counselors have less control over what takes place in the community and home than in the school, there are certain factors we need to be aware of in order to do our work most effectively. If students of poverty are not succeeding in school, it may be due to a variety of factors that affect academic achievement, such as poor nutrition, substandard housing, and substance abuse. These conditions influence students' ability to learn.

Another community factor is the legacy of discrimination that plagues many communities and affects the belief that one can or cannot succeed. The belief that some children cannot learn at high levels persists, and when children believe that society does not expect them to succeed, or when they themselves believe they cannot succeed, they do poorly in school.

In general, children-of-color and low-income children are less likely than White children to have parents with high levels of educational attainment. Combined with lower family income and parents' hectic work schedules, the extent to which parents can foster positive opportunities for learning at home is limited. Opportunities such as having access to books and computers—or even being read to before bedtime—may be more limited for ethnically diverse and low-income children. Finally, a family speaking a language other than English at home can also affect a child's learning opportunities.

Student Factors

There has been some research to indicate that low-income and culturally and linguistically diverse students' emotional and social development contributes to their low achievement. For instance, some research has suggested that African American students can become anxious about displaying negative racial stereotypes in their academic work. The result, researchers say, is a kind of vicious cycle in which African American students can be so worried about seeming stereotypically ungifted academically that their anxiety actually makes them perform less well than they could. This phenomenon has been called *stereotype threat* (Steele, 1997).

Peer pressure and identity issues have also been cited as contributing to the low academic achievement of culturally and linguistically diverse students. Peer pressure may cause students to ridicule or demean academic success. There is some dispute as to the effects of peer pressure, however. Some researchers (e.g., Ogbu, 1994), for example, have pointed to a phenomenon in high-minority schools whereby black students who perform poorly actually criticize their academically successful peers for "acting White." These researchers have charged that African American students tend to idolize a youth culture that scorns academic achievement. However, other researchers (Connell, Spencer, & Aber, 1994) have argued that such a culture exerts no special power on African American students in particular; instead, they claim that African American students are no more likely to dislike or scorn school than are White students.

WHAT DO WE KNOW ABOUT CLOSING THE GAP?

In 2000, the North Central Regional Education Laboratory (NCREL) published a study of high-performing, high-poverty schools in Wisconsin (Manset et al., 2000). They found that these schools had some common characteristics. Each had more than one of the following:

1. purposeful and proactive leadership,

2. data-based decision making and program monitoring,

3. a sense of community,

4. high expectations for students,

5. staff-initiated professional development,

6. opportunities for staff interaction,

7. curriculum aligned with state standards,

8. use of local and state assessment data,

9. parent and community involvement, and

10. alternative support programs.

In addition, several other studies have identified commonalities among successful schools. One of the federal Comprehensive School Reform models,

Success for All (Slavin et al., 1998) identified the following characteristics of schools that were instrumental in closing the gap:

1. leadership,

2. commitment of entire staff,

3. extensive professional development,

4. early literacy support, and

5. data-driven instructional decision-making and student monitoring.

This research points to common practices that show potential for closing the achievement gap. Leadership that establishes a culture of high expectations is certainly key. An emphasis on time for academic learning both during and beyond the school day is another policy and practice that works. In addition, schoolwide use of data and parental involvement seem to be critical components of schools that are successful.

Though this research is helpful, it is unclear how these school reform components translate to school counselor practice. The only current national school reform initiative that includes school counselors is the Education Trust's *Transforming School Counseling Initiative,* which focuses on the work of school counselors as advocates, leaders, and as creators of opportunities for all students to define, nurture, and accomplish high academic aspirations. The Education Trust has worked with a small percentage of counselor education programs on training "transformed school counselors."

Nevertheless, there is still much to be done to prepare counselors to work within a school reform framework. Without a doubt, school counselors can assist with school reform efforts by addressing issues of social justice through development of a school counseling program aligned with the American School Counselor Association's National Model and Standards. The social justice–focused functions offered in this book will hopefully begin to fill a void in the literature and in the work of school counselors.

Counselor in Action

Download data from your state's Department of Education Web site. Choose a school in an urban, suburban, and rural district. Examine each school's standardized test scores, attendance, dropouts, and graduation rates. Discuss with your colleagues the achievement gaps and any other gaps that you can detect in the data.

QUESTIONS TO CONSIDER

1. Why do you think school counselors and school counseling professionals have been absent from school reform initiatives?

2. How do you explain the lack of a gap between Asian American students and White students in reading and math?

3. In your community, what efforts are being made to close the achievement gap between students? Write down a few that come to mind. Are these efforts successful? Why or why not?

2 School Counseling Within the Context of Social Justice

Injustice anywhere is a threat to justice everywhere.

—Martin Luther King, Jr.

Issues of social justice are as relevant today as ever before. Questions of how to establish and, if necessary, enforce standards of fairness and ethical behavior arise in connection with virtually every pressing social and policy issue of our day. How do we manage the escalating threat of terrorism while protecting individual liberties and fostering religious and political equity? How can we build cooperation to arrive at fair and just resolutions of intergroup conflict? And, for school counselors, what are the best ways to ensure fair opportunities for, and respectful treatment of all students, regardless of ethnic, cultural, gender, or income group?

The question of counseling and social justice has engaged many counseling professionals, educators, and other scholars. Loretta Bradley chose social justice and advocacy as the thematic focus of her term (1999–2000) as president of the American Counseling Association (ACA). And in an address to the American Psychological Association's 2000 annual conference, the Reverend

Jesse Jackson reminded psychologists of Dr. Martin Luther King, Jr.'s charge to professionals in the field 30 years earlier (King, 1968). Jackson explained King's view that the social sciences are instruments of change and that, to this end, psychologists and counselors should "question the precepts of society, and reject those that permit injustice to form and grow" (Jackson, 2000, p. 328). And, in 2001, Kiselica and Robinson wrote a groundbreaking article which outlined the history, counselor attributes, skills, costs, pitfalls, rewards, and ethical issues associated with advocacy and social justice counseling.

REDEFINING SCHOOL COUNSELING TO SERVE DIVERSE GROUPS

A similar movement is evident with regard to school counseling. Lee (2005) emphasized that schools must be willing to redefine traditional counseling models and roles in order to serve diverse groups of students. Bemak and Chung (2005) and Green and Keys (2001) have also contributed to recent debates on these issues. They view social justice as an approach to school counseling based on (a) the acknowledgment of broad, systematic societal inequities and oppression, and (b) the assumption of the inevitable, if unintentional, location of every individual (and the profession) within this system. In turn, this assumption leads the school counselor to take responsible action that contributes to the elimination of systematic oppression in the forms of racism, sexism, heterosexism, classism, and other biases. This concept is closely related to multiculturalism, with its emphasis on cultural, racial, and ethnic issues, one of which is social injustice and oppression. As such, school counselors who believe in providing socially just school environments are expanding their definition of multicultural, or culturally diverse, counseling to include examining the way in which there is an *un*equal system in place in our schools and communities based on race and ethnicity and other cultural factors.

FOCUSING ON SOCIAL JUSTICE

Social justice refers to the idea of a just society, which gives individuals and groups their due. Social justice as a general concept is based on the idea of human rights. Thus, a broad definition of social justice would be *the way in which human rights are manifested in the everyday lives of people at every level of society.* Whereas equal opportunity and human rights are applicable to everyone, social justice targets the marginalized groups of people in society—it focuses on the disadvantaged. Social justice recognizes that there are situations in which application of the same rules to unequal groups can generate unequal results. Social justice provides a framework to assess the impact of policies and practices.

Multicultural counseling, on the other hand, refers to counseling in which the counselor and client take into account their cultural and personal experiences (Lee & Richardson, 1991). The focus of multicultural counseling is on the counseling process between two or more individuals who have different and distinct perceptions of the world. Typically, counselors who engage in effective multicultural counseling will promote social justice and will attend to the human rights of their clients.

After studying definitions of social justice and the work of Freire (1970), Sue, Arredondo, and McDavis (1992), Kiselica and Robinson (2001), Lee (1995), and Prilleltensky (1994), among others, I believe the following set of assumptions are important to keep in mind when developing a school counseling program that values and works toward social justice:

- The status quo is characterized by inequitable distribution of power and resources.
- External sources and factors influence individual behavior and attitudes.
- We have internalized the attitudes, understandings, and patterns of thoughts that allow us to function in and collaborate with systems of oppression.

All forms of oppression, such as racism, classism, ableism (prejudice against those with disabilities), sexism, and heterosexism, clearly undermine the emotional and interpersonal well-being of students and thus potentially result in student underachievement and mental and emotional distress. A social justice perspective acknowledges the role that dominant cultural values have in shaping the educational success and failure of youngsters, as evidenced by the achievement gap. Recognition, then, of the cultural implications of traditional school counseling practice and theory encourages counselors to consider ways in which societal structure and the status quo either privileges them and their students or puts them at a disadvantage. As a result, school counselors will be better able to understand their students' needs and help them achieve not only academically but socially, emotionally, and psychologically. Essentially, a social justice approach to school counseling is centered on reducing the effects of oppression on students and improving equity and access to educational services. Table 2.1 presents differences between what might be considered traditional school counseling and a social justice approach to school counseling.

Table 2.1 Traditional Versus Social Justice Approach in School Counseling

Traditional School Counseling	Social Justice Approach to School Counseling
Dependence on counseling theories and approaches with little to no regard for cultural background of students	Major focus of counseling is on highlighting the strengths of students (empowerment-based counseling)
Emphasis on individual student factors (e.g., unmotivated, depressed, angry)	Emphasis on sociocultural and environmental factors (e.g., poverty, discrimination) that influence students' behavior and performance
Little to no emphasis on oppression and its influence on students	Major goal of school counseling program is to challenge oppression and oppressive practices in schools
Emphasis on equality	Emphasis on equality and equity
School counseling activities typically implemented during the school day	School counseling activities implemented during the school day *and* after school hours (e.g., advocating for policies, resources) in the community
Reliance on labels to identify students (e.g., "defiant," "aggressive")	Avoidance of labeling. Students are described by their strengths and positive characteristics
Little to no use of data to guide programming or to evaluate services	Dependence on data to guide counseling services and to evaluate existing interventions
Focus on maintaining the status quo	Focus on changing existing policies and strategies so that all students are successful
Focus on enrolling students in "comfortable" courses	Focus on enrolling students in more rigorous courses

Oppression and Anti-Oppression Education

Oppression refers to a social dynamic in which certain ways of being in this world—including certain ways of identifying or being identified—are normalized or privileged while other ways are oppressed or marginalized. Forms of oppression include racism, classism, sexism, heterosexism, anti-Semitism, and ableism, among others. More specifically, oppression occurs in situations in which people are exploited, marginalized, or rendered powerless (Zutlevics, 2002). A faulty belief that people tend to subscribe to is that those who are oppressed are somehow "less than" or inferior to those who are not oppressed. *Internalized oppression* is the manner in which an oppressed group ironically comes to use against itself the methods of the oppressor.

Anti-oppressive education encourages us to critically analyze our commonsense methods to see if they somehow contribute to the perpetuation of oppression. What results is a deep commitment to changing how we think about and engage in many aspects of education, from curriculum and pedagogy, to school culture and activities, to institutional structure and policies. Ideally, educators will make a commitment to exploring perspectives that do not conform to what has become common sense in the field of education. Anti-oppressive education aims to challenge the status quo at the risk of being controversial and causing discomfort.

Equity Versus Equality

Arthur Levine, President of Columbia University's Teachers College, stated in the school's 2004 annual report that "The equity issue should be as important to education schools as AIDS or cancer is to medical schools" (Teachers College Columbia University, 2004, p. 3). I agree with Dr. Levine's statement and firmly believe that equity is at the core of a social justice approach to school counseling. At its most fundamental level, equity is an orientation toward doing the right thing by students (Marshall, 2002), which does not mean treating students equally regardless of their different needs. Imagine communities in which one's race, ethnicity, or culture is not the most powerful predictor of how one fares. In a racially equitable community, some children excel in school and some struggle—but race isn't the factor that makes the difference. Some families are wealthy and some are poor—and there are people of every race at both ends of the wealth spectrum, and in the middle. A community in which individuals and groups have racial-ethnic and cultural identities, but those racial and ethnic identities do not predict whether an adolescent goes to college or jail or which groups are healthiest and how long they are likely to live on average.

Equity requires that school counselors treat students differently on the basis of aspects of the students' cultures, including race, ethnicity, gender, and economic class. However, decisions to treat students differently should always be based on students' specific needs. Equity demands that school counselors resist using aspects of culture or external factors (e.g., poverty, family status, disability) as excuses for not setting high standards and demanding the best of students. In short, equity forces school counselors and educators to focus on students' strengths, not their deficits.

Equality, in contrast urges counselors and educators to enforce formal school policies in a consistent manner. Equality focuses on impartiality and retaining policies without regard to student differences or unique circumstances. Ideally, counselors and other educators should seek a balance between equity and equality in their school practices because both are critical to promoting success for all students. However, it is important to remember that school policies that are grounded in equity bring about different results than those that are based on equality. For example, a school may enforce their zero-tolerance discipline policy in terms of equality. However, when examining the data regarding the students who have been expelled because of the policy, school officials may realize that the policy is more detrimental to, say, Native American boys when executed equally. From an equity perspective, the school would then need to reevaluate its discipline policy and the core issues (e.g., low teacher expectations, tardiness) that are at the root of discipline problems among Native American boys. It could then develop a new discipline policy and train the staff to use a new discipline curriculum that includes more culturally appropriate discipline strategies.

Resource A features a list of questions that should be discussed by a school's leadership team to assess whether or not equity is being addressed by the school.

Counseling Snapshot

Scenario I

At Jones Middle School, seventh-grade students were frequently given math homework that required calculator and computer usage. The math teachers assumed that all of the students had access to computers and calculators. A majority of the students did have computers and calculators at home, but a small percentage (5%) did not and, as a result, received lower grades on their math homework. The 5% who scored lowest on math assessments were primarily from low-socioeconomic and Native American backgrounds. One of the school counselors pointed out this inequitable practice to the seventh-grade math teachers. As a result, when assigned homework required computer or calculator usage, teachers would permit students to use computers during their study period and to borrow calculators from the school. (EQUITY)

(Continued)

(Continued)

Scenario 2

Jamal, a high school counselor in an urban district, realized that students in the magnet program at his school were not being held to the same discipline standards as the students in the general population. He collected data that showed that—for the same offense—students in the magnet program were not issued the same punishment as students in the general population. As a result of Jamal's presentation of this data, the administration developed a new schoolwide discipline policy that they enforced equally with all students. (EQUALITY)

Ask Yourself

Does the following scenario present an equity or equality issue?

At your high school, 62% of graduating seniors are offered admission to a 4-year college or university. The most recent data indicate that only 5% of the students offered admission to 4-year colleges and universities are students-of-color (students-of-color make up 43% of the school's population). After further review of data, you discover that students-of-color are disproportionately underrepresented in courses that are required for college admission, such as calculus and advanced placement English.

Is this an equity or equality issue? Why or why not? What would you do to ensure equity and equality in this case?

KEY FUNCTIONS OF SCHOOL COUNSELING BASED ON A SOCIAL JUSTICE APPROACH

The following section outlines what I believe are six key functions (the six C's) of school counselors who employ a social justice approach in their work. (See Figure 2.1 on page 23.) The key functions include

1. counseling and intervention planning;

2. consultation;

3. connecting schools, families, and communities;

4. collecting and utilizing data;

5. challenging bias; and

6. coordinating student services and support.

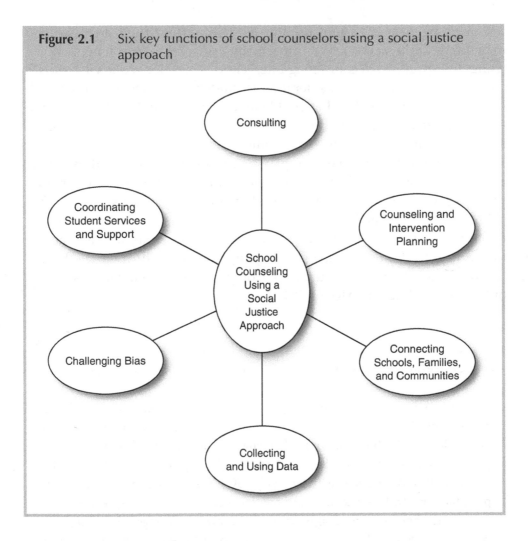

Figure 2.1 Six key functions of school counselors using a social justice approach

Counseling and Intervention Planning

This function includes implementing counseling and interventions that acknowledge and integrate students' cultural and familial issues. The importance of school counselors being able to identify and recognize both the academic and personal or social needs of marginalized youth is critical. School counselor strategies for assessing and assisting students with emotional and psychological problems should be tailored to meet the specific needs of specific student populations. For instance, depression and anxiety-related problems, frequently observed in poor and minority communities, are often overlooked. Emphasis should be placed on students within their environment, sometimes referred to as the *person-in-environment approach*. This focus takes into account students' background experiences, their interaction with others in their families and immediate community, the resources in their environment, and most important their adaptive and maladaptive interactions with other people in their environment. When using this approach to counseling interventions, a school counselor should consider giving special consideration to students' particular cultural values. By doing so, she'll be better able to identify student problems within environmental and personal contexts and better able to refer students to specific community assistance programs, if relevant.

Counseling and intervention planning is ideally carried out by school counselors who are culturally competent. Cultural competence, broadly speaking, involves combining cultural awareness and sensitivity with a skill set that, together, bring about effective cross-cultural practices (Diller & Moule, 2004). To assess your cultural knowledge, awareness, and ability to work with culturally diverse students and staff, turn to the School Counselor Multicultural Counseling Competence Checklist in Resource B of this book (Holcomb-McCoy, 2004).

Counseling Snapshot

Jameel is a sixth-grade African American student at your school. Jameel's older brother was recently murdered in a drug transaction outside his home. There has been an overwhelming amount of media coverage and Jameel's brother has been characterized as a "drug dealer" and "thug." The school counselor has met with Jameel for 30 minutes on a daily basis to support him and to listen to his fears and feelings. The counselor realizes that Jameel has become more aggressive, withdrawn, and angry. Believing that Jameel is suffering from depression, she consults with a local therapist specializing in depression among African American adolescents. The counselor, in consultation with the therapist, develop a treatment plan for Jameel. At the same time, the counselor works with community agencies to provide Jameel's family with the support they need during this period.

Consultation

The consultation function involves school counselors meeting with a student's parents and teachers to discuss the student without the student present in an effort to address issues of student equity, access, and success. Consultation, unlike counseling, is an indirect service delivery approach, and can be used to influence change in an entire classroom, school, or family. Counselors can use consultation as a means to support parents, teachers and students most appropriately so that they can better assist students, particularly low-achieving or at-risk students. It is through the role of consultant that a school counselor can serve as an advocate for students who are being either treated unfairly or are unable to speak for themselves. Important roles include

- identifying school or student inequities during the consultation process with teachers, parents, and other educators;
- ongoing consultation with teachers and community members to educate them about how they can best support all students;
- attention to the cross-cultural nature of student-to-teacher interactions in teacher consultation;
- attention to teacher and parent self-awareness in consultation.

Counseling Snapshot

A young female teacher has a reputation for sending at least one Latino male student to the office every day for discipline purposes. The principal addresses the matter with the teacher and asks the counselor to help by consulting with the teacher. Through several consultation meetings with the teacher, the counselor becomes aware of the teacher's negative stereotypes and assumptions about Latino men. In consultation, the counselor states her concerns about the teacher's biased attitudes toward Latino males.

Connecting Schools, Families, and Communities

Time is a precious commodity for all school-based educators. To the extent that they are able, school counselors should try to spend as much time as possible listening and working in partnership with the community and families of students to improve services offered in the school. When working in this role, it is beneficial if counselors can be flexible and collaborative. By presenting relevant programming to the community on cultural diversity and social justice issues, counselors can promote an understanding of the impact of oppression on students' psychological and educational development. School-family-community partnerships have proven to be effective in raising the test scores of culturally and linguistically diverse and low-income students (Bohan-Baker & Little, 2002).

> **Counseling Snapshot**
>
> A middle school's community has experienced a series of hate crimes targeting the influx of gay couples in one of its neighborhoods. The hate crimes have caused many students and parents to fear coming into the school. Many parents worry that their children may get hurt. The counselor initiates a committee of concerned parents, community members (including gay couples in the community), representatives from the police department, and school personnel. The committee's goal is to develop a plan for ceasing the hate crimes and educating the community on gay issues and concerns.

Collecting and Using Data

Data help us make critical decisions related to inequities and social injustices that occur in the school and evaluate existing counseling interventions. Data collection increases a school counselor's ability to monitor student progress and to understand which students may need more guidance or intervention. Counselors can better highlight social injustices and advocate for students and families by collecting, analyzing, and presenting data to colleagues. We can collect data pertaining to student test scores, attendance, dropout rates, suspension, expulsion, and grades. By analyzing the results, we are better able to discover achievement and opportunity gaps categorized by grade, race, immigrant status, income status, gender, disability, or any cultural specification.

> **Counseling Snapshot**
>
> One of the school counselors at Saint Francis High School collected data indicating that 12% of eleventh-grade students drop out before graduation. Further analysis of the data showed that those who dropped out were primarily made up of African American and Latino girls: 42% of the students who drop out are African American girls and 50% are Latino girls. The counselor presented her data to the administration and her school counseling colleagues. After much discussion, they decided to present the data to the entire high school staff so that a plan of action could be developed.

Challenging Bias

One of the most important functions of a school counselor within a social justice framework is to challenge bias and oppressive behavior (both intentional and unintentional) in the school setting and community. Clearly, bias and prejudice can inhibit student achievement and influence the behavior and perceptions of educators. For this reason, we need to be diligent about identifying and challenging our own biases and those of others. We can then help to shape new policies that eliminate biased or oppressive practices. We can also incorporate social justice education into the work we do with students as a means of challenging their biases.

Counseling Snapshot

Tim, an elementary school counselor, is a member of the site-based leadership team at his school. During the selection process of a parent committee member, several committee members mentioned that the committee should choose a parent who is a stay-at-home mother because she would be available for meetings and would understand the mission of the school. Tim opposed this idea and challenged the committee's bias about who should participate on the leadership team. He felt that the committee was not giving all parents an opportunity to participate in an important and powerful aspect of the school.

Coordinating Student Services

The research suggests that far too often, poor and ethnically diverse students encounter watered-down curricula and unchallenging academic environments. Providing students with counseling and additional supports to encourage and enhance their learning is important. Counselors can collaborate with organizations and institutions (e.g., local universities, civic groups), that can provide these extra supports for students' academic and emotional development. School counselors who work from a social justice framework focus on providing support for the low-income and ethnically diverse students underrepresented in rigorous classes such as advanced placement courses. Also, school counselors can also use scheduling and other counselor activities (career and job fair coordination, Individualized Education Program meetings, etc.) in advocating for student access to activities and programs that would further advance all students' potential for attending college and for other advanced opportunities.

Counseling Snapshot

Dawn, a high school counselor, has developed an ongoing relationship with staff in the local university's career center. She and the director of the career center have developed a series of student workshops for juniors and seniors from underrepresented groups (e.g., African American, Latino, Native American) at the university. The university provides transportation for the students to travel to campus and they provide materials that can assist parents with the college application and tuition process.

QUESTIONS TO CONSIDER

1. How would you handle a situation in which you want to challenge a particular bias that your fellow counselors are not willing to recognize?

2. Social justice is often defined as providing fairness and equality for all. Do you think it is possible for all students to be treated equally in a school?

3 Counseling and Intervention Planning

The shoe that fits one person pinches another; there is no recipe for living that suits all cases.

—Carl Jung

While presenting on the topic of school counseling for social justice, a middle school counselor asked: "Are you saying that school counselors should stop doing counseling? It sounds like you want counselors to do more 'academic' work than 'counseling' work. Isn't that going backwards?" Dumbfounded, I responded, "Is there a school counselor who is not doing academic work? All counseling that occurs in schools *is* related to the academic development of students."

Although the goal of my presentation was to challenge counselors to be more active in equity issues, advocacy, and systemic types of work, I did not intend for the group to think that counseling was not a major part of their role in schools. Counseling is still needed in schools and students benefit greatly from counseling experiences. However, there is far too much counseling taking place that is culturally inappropriate. I believe that the counseling taking place in schools should be more culturally appropriate and empowerment focused. School counselors who work from a social justice perspective use strategies that enhance students' sense of self-worth, academic and personal self-efficacy, and ultimately enhance students' feelings of empowerment. The challenge for counselors is to initiate counseling with a keen understanding of equity, a knowledge of the barriers to effective cross-cultural counseling, and an ability to build on the strengths of students and their families

After I explained the ways in which social justice can underlie the counseling function, the school counselor in the scenario above was more receptive to what I had to say. However, she was still unsure of how to do it. There is no cookbook for how to implement counseling that will empower or create the change necessary for students to achieve. However, I told her that if she can start from the point of asking herself the following questions, she will be moving in the right direction:

- What are the strengths of this student?
- What survival skills have this student or the student's family used to get to this point?
- What environmental barriers need to be removed to help this student be successful? How can I—or we—alter that environment?

This chapter offers ways to take a social justice approach to counseling and intervention planning. Because counseling is the cornerstone of school counseling programs, it is often this area in which counselors feel most comfortable. Part of delivering effective counseling services is developing cultural competence and the ability to work with students sensitively, creatively, and responsibly. This also includes taking into account the societal and environmental factors that influence students' success.

CRITICAL FACTORS THAT AFFECT SCHOOL COUNSELING AND THE COUNSELING RELATIONSHIP

Culture

Assimilation—or the degree to which cultural groups are able to blend into the "norm"—was once the expectation for culturally diverse people in the United States. As a result, assimilation involved hiding or even rejecting one's cultural uniqueness. Today our society is increasingly recognizing and appreciating the value of cultural diversity and the importance of helping students navigate social, academic, and career ladders while retaining their cultural uniqueness. Because this was not the case for many years, however, many students-of-color and others from culturally diverse backgrounds still feel that their culture is not valued by school systems, and rightly so in many cases. We see this particularly in the way many students avoid voluntarily meeting with or opening up to school counselors.

Cultural differences and cultural group membership can have a significant influence on the behaviors of school counselors and students. During counseling, cultural differences and expectations can influence how a counselor perceives a student and how a student perceives a counselor. In many cases, school counselors think that when they treat all students the same that they are being fair and culturally sensitive. Although the intent is right, this practice is problematic because all students are not the same. Students, particularly those from historically oppressed groups, have different needs, experiences, and perceptions. Therefore, students' cultural backgrounds will likely determine the way in which they approach counseling, perceive their counselor, and react to the content of what a school counselor says. For instance, a 14-year-old Muslim student may become agitated and anxious when the counselor assumes that all students go to church on Sunday. Or an African American female student in a predominately White school could become angry and resistant to counseling if a White counselor described beauty as "fair skin with keen features" in a group counseling session. Being sensitive to cultural differences during counseling is imperative and forms the basis for students' perceptions of school counselors.

Prejudice, Discrimination, and Oppression

To someone who has not experienced prejudice, discrimination, and oppression, it is difficult to convey fully the insidious, pervasive, and lifelong impact that they can have. In addition to affecting the way a person perceives him- or herself, these experiences also influence the way in which a person relates to others.

Students' academic and social development intersects with the effects of class, religion, geographic region, migration status, sexual orientation, gender, and experiences of prejudice and discrimination. Allport (1954) defined prejudice as *beliefs based on faulty and inflexible generalizations*. Attitudes originating from these beliefs may be directed toward a group as a whole or toward an individual because he or she is a member of that group. The group or individual who becomes the object of prejudice most often experiences a position of disadvantage.

The potential to experience the social stressors of prejudice and discrimination exists for culturally diverse students. For example, Malik, age 10, reported to his counselor, "My teacher doesn't like Black people; that's why I don't do her work. She never calls on Black kids, and I heard her say that kids from the projects don't learn good." Or, Sam, age 16, reported to a teacher, "My counselor told me that I could never go to that University because no kids from my neighborhood have ever been accepted there." Sam's teacher apparently nodded and agreed with the counselor, thus sending Sam the message that he should not apply to that college based on his socioeconomic status. Other culturally diverse groups share the brunt of similar comments. School counselors who want to build a relationship of trust and openness with students need to acknowledge the effects of prejudice and discrimination, and approach the counseling relationship mindfully.

Discomfort and Fear

Not only should school counselors assess the impact of other people's prejudiced beliefs on students' achievement, but they must also be cognizant of their own prejudiced beliefs that cause them to fear and feel uncomfortable with certain groups of students. Without a doubt, a counselor's fear and discomfort will interfere with the counseling relationship. The following example illustrates this point:

> William, a 16-year-old student, went to his school counselor to discuss his painful experience of coming out to his parents. He expressed sadness and anger that his family openly "put him down" because of his sexual orientation. As the counselor listened to him talk, however, she had a difficult time suppressing her own surprise that William was gay. Hoping to learn more, she said, "Oh, I didn't know you were gay. When did that happen?" William, in turn, was put off by her comment and sat silently, unresponsive. The counselor waited for a response while shuffling papers on her desk. After a few minutes, William said he had to go, and walked out. He never spoke to the counselor again.

The counselor in this example would have done better to simply ask William more about his feelings, and not pry about his process of coming to understand his sexual orientation. But even if a student does not come to the counselor to talk about a cultural issue specifically, counselors should ask themselves the following questions about their treatment of culturally diverse students in all of the work they do:

- Am I equally comfortable working with all students (e.g., gay and straight students, students from different religious groups, students of various ethnic backgrounds)?
- If not, are there certain services I may be denying to students because of my own level of discomfort?
- How might I or my fellow counselors reach these students so that they have access to the services to which all students are entitled?

In working with culturally diverse students, a different issue can present itself. Some counselors may hold an unrecognized fear of the potential dangerousness of the student on the basis of stereotypes and a lack of familiarity with the particular cultural background. Norris and Spurlock (1992) reported that counselors with limited contact or direct experience with people of a particular culture may initiate counseling with fears that stem from prejudices and stereotypes. School counselors may even distance themselves from students by passively accepting a student's refusal to meet or talk with them. It's important, then, for counselors to separate the student from the stereotype, and put fears aside in favor of doing right by all students. In the Suggested Readings at the end of the book, there are a number of resources I recommend that discuss prejudice, discrimination, and oppression. I encourage reading as many of these books as possible, individually or in a study group with other school counselors. The optimal environment to discuss this reading should be a comfortable space with few distractions. In the optimal setting, each small group should have a trained facilitator who is experienced in issues of prejudice, discrimination, and oppression.

Migration and Acculturation

Many culturally diverse students are immigrants, either recently or in the past, or are the children of parents who immigrated. For those who have recently migrated, it is helpful for school counselors to understand the reasons and circumstances for the migration, which family members came and which didn't (and why), and the level of disruption this caused in the child's supportive system. For some, the process may have been voluntary, the families having chosen to come for better educational and job opportunities in a receptive host community. For others, who may have escaped war-torn countries where they may have experienced the loss of their loved ones and the chronic disruption of other supportive networks such as their extended families and schools, this process may be different. The Suggested Readings at the back of the book offers information on numerous resources that address migration and acculturation to help school counselors understand these important factors.

Social Class

Research indicates that poverty rates among American children have reached as high as 22% in recent years, and from this historically elevated figure, perhaps a third can be described as experiencing "persistent" or "long-term" poverty (Brady, 2003). It is widely believed that children from low-income backgrounds pose a major challenge to schools. Many reside in inner cities or relatively isolated rural areas, compounding existing obstacles to equal educational opportunities and academic success. Yet, studies consistently document that most educators, including school counselors, come from middle-class backgrounds, making it difficult for them to relate personally with students who live in poverty (Zeichner, 2003).

Among the many factors that are related to a student's lived experience, social class or socioeconomic status seems to be the least understood. However, as society changes and social class issues become more prominent, school counselors must consider the influence of social class or economic status on the lives and experiences of students. More important, school counselors must consider students' resources based on their socioeconomic background and how the lack of resources can create inequities in students' opportunities and access. A list of readings on social class and counseling can be found in the Suggested Reading section at the back of the book.

Language Differences

Language differences present another perceived obstacle for school counselors. If the counselor is not bilingual or has limited proficiency in the primary language of the student, the language barrier can affect the student-counselor relationship. If the counselor does not clearly understand what the student is trying to communicate, for example, she may unintentionally recommend an inappropriate intervention. It is also possible that the student may spend so much time trying to say words correctly in order to be understood that he or she may not accurately reflect his or her feelings and behaviors to the counselor. (Gopaul-McNicol & Thomas-Presswood, 1998). Therefore, counselors of bilingual students should achieve some level of proficiency in the student's primary language. Short of this, they should do their best to bring another trusted person into the counseling session who can interpret the idiosyncrasies, subtle nuances, and idiomatic expressions in the student's primary language. Ideally, another counselor or a school professional could serve in this position. School counselors working to achieve equity for all should be able to admit their limitations in working with bilingual students and do their best to find a solution that will work for both them and the students being served. Bilingualism and counseling resources are listed in the Suggested Readings section at the end of the book.

CULTURALLY APPROPRIATE COUNSELING INTERVENTIONS

In the previous sections of this chapter, I have introduced how a variety of factors have an impact on the counseling process. In this section, I will address methods to help school counselors provide culturally sensitive and appropriate counseling for diverse groups of students.

Helping Students Process Their Behavior, Attitudes, and Feelings

Beyond acknowledging their own uncertainties, fears, fixed notions, and stereotypes, counselors have a responsibility to acknowledge students' negative feelings and attitudes. Helping students process their behavior, attitudes, and feelings about counseling and school-related issues is something school counselors can do to show their respect for students, and demonstrate that they genuinely accept students for who they are, even if they must work together to improve a particular behavior or attitude. If the school counselor addresses issues that she recognizes may affect the counseling relationship, difficulties will be avoided. The following story illustrates this point:

> Elissa, a 16-year-old student, went to her counselor to discuss her schedule for the next semester. Since arriving at the high school the previous year, Elissa had never been to her counselor's office. Because Elissa's grades were in the average to above average range, the counselor had never requested to speak to her. However, when Elissa signed up for Honors Trigonometry, the counselor wanted to make sure that she was aware of the challenging nature of the course.
>
> In the conference with the school counselor, Elissa was quiet and reserved. She did not look at the counselor and her arms were crossed throughout the conference. She nodded in agreement with everything that the counselor said. The counselor finally asked, "Elissa, I detect that you are a bit nervous talking to me. Is this true?" Elissa nodded in agreement, and so the counselor continued: "What makes you nervous about talking to me?" Elissa didn't speak, but the counselor went on to acknowledge that it's sometimes scary to come to the guidance office. She reassured Elissa that she wanted to help her have a positive school experience and would be open to listen to any of her concerns. Elissa smiled and left the office. The following week, Elissa returned, wanting to talk with her counselor about changing a course.

This type of simple exchange between a counselor and student can be particularly powerful. The ability to build trust and respect between the counselor and student is critical to counseling programs that take a social justice approach. The example with Elissa nicely demonstrates the early stages of the three components of the effective counseling relationship:

working alliance, transference-countertransference, and real relationship (Terrell & Cheatham, 1996).

The *working alliance* is the alignment that occurs between the counselor and student. The counselor acts as a positive mirror for the student, reflecting the student as a unique and valuable individual. This positive reflection allows the student to see himself as an individual *with* an issue (such as a concern or problem), rather than *as* the issue. More important, the counselor is an ally or advocate who can help the student resolve external and internal conflicts. For example, a low-income fourth-grade student, whose father was recently incarcerated and whose mother is struggling to support five children and adolescents, is acting out in class and not turning in homework. His school counselor realizes that he may not need a study skills or anger management group but rather needs to discuss his struggles at home in a safe, nonjudgmental environment. This culturally sensitive and appropriate intervention places the counselor in the role of trusted advocate.

Transference is the unconscious process by which students' negative feelings, attitudes, and behaviors that are associated with discriminatory practices are transferred onto the counselor. Similarly, *countertransference* or *counselor transference* is the counselor's responses to the student that stem from the counselor's past relationships and experiences. Elissa, for example, may have associated going to the counselor's office with being "in trouble" and for that reason was closed-off and quiet. Counselor transference could have occurred if the counselor had a preconceived notion about "students like Elissa" (say, those who seemed shy or resistant) and assumed that Elissa would be the same. Using the example of the fourth grader mentioned previously, countertransference might play out if the counselor validates his or her faulty perceptions (based on his or her past experiences with low-income fourth-grade students) by stating, "If you would only listen to your teachers and do your work, everything would get better. Stop being lazy." It is important that school counselors recognize transference and countertransference because both are important to understanding the dynamics of counseling and both are essential to the counseling relationship.

The *real relationship* operates from a genuineness, respect, authenticity, and openness that both counselor and student have established. These positive relationship qualities may be hampered by misconceptions, prejudiced beliefs, lack of cultural knowledge, and lack of self-awareness. The school counselor who genuinely wants equitable treatment for all students must begin to obtain knowledge regarding different types of cultures and issues in diverse communities. In addition, the school counselor should be willing to participate in different environments that provide a working knowledge and awareness of culturally diverse people. Thus, counselors who examine their culturally based attitudes and beliefs and who are self-aware are capable of developing a real relationship with all students. Listening, interpreting, appreciating students' differences through appropriate verbal and nonverbal responses, and identifying pertinent student issues, amplifies the school counselor's ability to form real relationships. Please refer to the Suggested Readings later in this book for a list of titles on multicultural counseling relationships that I strongly recommend counselors read and digest.

Strengths-Based Counseling

Strengths-based counseling assesses and recognizes the inherent strengths of students, and then builds on those strengths to create change (Ungar, 2006; Wong, 2006). Strengths-based counseling is highly effective when working with students-of-color or students who have a history of being marginalized in the school. The focus of counseling when using a strengths perspective is not on "fixing a broken student" or on fixing a problem. Instead the focus is on determining student strengths and emphasizing those strengths to resolve or at least reduce the frequency of the problem that brought the student to the counselor's attention. The strengths-based approach reduces the power structure between the student and the counselor and it instills hope that the student has something positive to offer and achieve.

Effective strengths-based practice may require that school counselors acknowledge that they are not necessarily significant in the lives of students—that is, *they* are not going to produce the change in students' lives. Rather, school counselors act as a resource and a guide for students as they strive to change their lives themselves using their innate abilities. School counselors who use a strengths-based approach do not use stigmatizing labels and behavior descriptors to describe students. The following terms should never be used about students because they only further alienate students and negatively shape their realities:

- noncompliant
- resistive
- unwilling
- unmotivated
- poor insight
- dysfunctional
- oppositional
- defiant

A strengths-based approach requires that school counselors use students' strengths when discussing or describing student concerns. It also requires that school counselors point out their perceptions of students' strengths or ask students to identify their own strengths. In the following exchange, the school counselor reflects the student's concern in a way that highlights her existing strengths without trying to change her negative feelings.

Student: I stayed in the advanced math class even though I hate math. I hate math and I hate that class!

Counselor: It sounds like you really dislike math, which makes me admire your perseverance.

School counselors and students might also collaborate to give meaningful labels to the identified strengths, as demonstrated in the conversation here between a school counselor and a fifth-grade student:

School counselor: Yesterday, your friends were making fun of you, yet you remained calm. What was it about you that helped you remain calm?

Student: I was really angry at my friends but I didn't want to get in trouble again. So, I just walked away.

School counselor: That ability you had to walk away when you were angry, can you give it a name? What would you call that?

Student: [*Thinks for a minute*] I'll call it my "no trouble strength" because I'm tired of going to the office and getting in trouble.

School counselor: Tell me more about when you use your "no trouble strength."

It is important that school counselors working from a social justice and strengths-based perspective avoid referring to students by a label or a diagnosis. For instance, describing a student as "hyper" or an "ADHD student" identifies the student as their diagnosis rather than as a person with a physical, emotional, or psychological difficulty. It is better to use what is called *person-first language,* which would mean that a school counselor works with "a student with ADHD" rather than "an ADHD student," or "a child with a reading disability" as opposed to "the reading-disabled kid." Recognizing the person first helps dissociate him or her from the diagnosis or problem being dealt with, and makes it easier to shift the focus to strengths. Counselors can use inherent character strengths to great success as a starting point for counseling and further growth.

Counseling Snapshot

Shameka, an African American seventh-grade student, went to the counselor with concerns about a failing math grade and complaints about her math teacher. Shameka has a label among teachers of being a "troublemaker." Teachers have written on her report cards that she "talks back," "does not respect authority," and "is too aggressive in her tone." Shameka receives grades in the C range but she scored extremely high on intelligence and gifted placement tests.

In the counselor's office, Shameka opens up about her home life. Born and raised in a low-income, inner city neighborhood, Shameka is the oldest of five children and she currently lives with her grandmother in a two-bedroom apartment. Shameka's mother is in and out of her life and she has had no contact with her father since she was 5 years old.

Because Shameka's grandmother is diabetic and very ill, Shameka is responsible for getting her younger siblings to school. Shameka says that she often thinks about what her life would be like if her mother and father were together. Shameka admits that she is angry with her parents because they are not around and she wishes that she had "another life." The school counselor expresses empathy for Shameka and focuses their time together on identifying the strengths she has relied on to survive and cope with her difficulties. The counselor identifies Shameka's intelligence, perseverance, and maturity. Shameka identifies her major strength as her unwillingness to take "stuff" from other people. The counselor calls it assertiveness. Shameka and her counselor continue to spend significant time planning how Shameka can use her strengths to work on her problems at school.

Empowerment-Based Counseling

Although traditional counseling theories and approaches (e.g., person-centered, rational emotive) can be modified and applied to counseling with most students, they still lack focus on issues pertaining to students' struggles with their environment or the impact of the environment on the students. For students and families who struggle to overcome decades of oppression and marginalization, they require more than what these traditional theories offer. Students-of-color and low-income students benefit from school counselors who are able to not only apply traditional counseling approaches but who are also skilled in advocacy and empowerment.

Empowerment and advocacy are not new to the counseling field. In the 1970s, the growth of community counseling brought advocacy and community organizing to the attention of the counseling profession (Toporek & Liu, 2001). The facilitation of changes in the student's environment was seen as a necessary and appropriate role for counselors. Although there has been an emergence of literature suggesting that school counselors should be advocates, for the most part, discussions of advocacy, empowerment, and social action have remained on the periphery.

Advocacy is defined as action taken by counselors to facilitate the removal of external and institutional barriers for students' well-being. Empowerment is at one end of the advocacy and is characterized by the counselor helping the student achieve goals with the ultimate outcome being to enable the student to act independently in the future. As a general definition, empowerment can be defined as a process of increasing personal, interpersonal, or political power so that individuals, families, and communities can take action to improve their situations. It is a process that fosters power (that is, the capacity to implement) in disenfranchised and powerless groups of people, for use in their own lives, their communities, and in their society, by acting on issues that they define as important.

When counseling, *critical consciousness* can be used to move students to a point at which they feel a sense of personal power (empowerment). Critical consciousness involves three psychological processes:

1. *group identification* that includes identifying areas of common experiences and concern with a particular group;

2. *group consciousness*, which involves understanding the differential status of power of groups in society; and

3. *self-and collective efficacy*, which is described as perceiving one's self as a subject (rather than object) of social processes and as capable of working to change the social order.

For students to understand that their problems stem from a lack of power, they must first comprehend their group's status in society as well as the overall structure of power in society. At the individual level, counselors can help students gain empowerment by facilitating discussions about one's group identification and helping them understand how their group membership has affected their life circumstances. Equipped with this greater understanding and with new confidence in themselves, students can develop new life strategies that better meet their needs.

Counseling Snapshot

Edward, a Native American 10th grader, is told to see the counselor because of recent confrontations with teachers. Edward tells the counselor that he is tired of being told what to do by "these f—g White teachers. They want to tell us what to do. . . . They are the problem. They go back to their nice families and nice houses, and leave us here . . . with crappy houses and nothing. I hate White people." The counselor recognizes Edward's anger and frustration with the oppression of his people. He validates Edward's anger, "I hear your anger and frustration with White people."

Ask Yourself

1. What could the counselor say next in order for Edward to explore his group's history of oppression?

2. How might you link his group's history to future empowerment? Practice what you would say with a friend or colleague.

Ethnic Identity Development and Counseling

For ethnic minority adolescents, their ethnicity can play an important role in their identity development. Jean Phinney (1990) proposed a three-stage model of ethnic identity development that includes a progression from an unexamined ethnic identity through a period of exploration to an achieved or committed ethnic identity. According to her model, early adolescents who have not been exposed to ethnic identity issues are in the first status, or *diffused ethnic identity*. This early stage is characterized by an adolescent's lack of active exploration of ethnic issues. A lack of interest or concern regarding ethnic issues manifests a diffused identity level. Phinney purported that early adolescents may simply not be interested in ethnicity and may have given it little thought. Alternatively, some adolescents may have made a commitment without exploration on the basis of inherited ethnic attitudes from parents or other influential adults. That is, their attitudes represent *a foreclosed status*. Adolescents with diffused and foreclosed statuses are at risk of accepting and internalizing negative and faulty stereotypes and beliefs. Phinney encourages the active exploration of one's ethnicity (*moratorium*) before reaching an *achieved identity*.

Social justice–focused school counselors are aware of the importance of adolescent ethnic identity development and they make enhancing students' ethnic and racial identity development a major priority when counseling.

In order to do this, school counselors recognize that the failure of an adolescent to examine ethnic issues and his or her ethnic identity creates risks for poor psychological and educational adjustment. In his clinical work, Zayas (2001) found that ethnic minority youth benefit from discussing their struggles with racism and ethnic identity. He found that adolescents' struggles with their ethnic identity were made salient when issues related to peer-group relations, family relations, and achievement were elicited. In this respect, providing students the opportunity to clarify, actively explore, and examine ethnic issues and their ethnic identity would enhance student development.

Group Counseling

Group work is one mode of counseling that has been indicated in the literature as a viable means to nurture adolescents' ethnic identity development (Baca & Koss-Chioino, 1997; Noam, 1999). Ethnic exploration groups in which students research their ethnic heritage, talk with others about their ethnic background, and learn new information about other cultures and ethnic groups can be implemented by school counselors to enhance students' ethnic identity development. An activity for a small group of eighth-grade Korean American middle school students might include completing the following: "Being Korean American in this community means ... ," and "Being Korean American in this school means. . . ." These types of activities can act as a catalyst for students' exploration of the meaning attached to their ethnicity and in turn, enhance their ethnic identity development.

In group work, counselors might also help early adolescents process others' negative perceptions about race and ethnicity (Holcomb-McCoy & Moore-Thomas, 2001). A Mexican American male group member, for example, complains to the counselor that students are teasing him because of his Mexican name and heritage. The counselor might encourage the student to discuss his feelings in relationship to the encounter and his feelings related to experiencing racism. Other group members should also have the opportunity to share similar experiences or to share how they would feel in a similar situation. These group discussions can ultimately lead to an exploration of students' feelings related to their ethnic membership. The counselor in this example might also guide the group in problem solving activities and help students determine ways to handle this situation or similar situations in the future. Role playing could be implemented to help students determine appropriate solutions to problems related to their ethnic group membership.

Examining Ethnic Identity With Uninterested Students

School counselors using a social justice approach are also prepared to work with students who lack an interest in exploring their ethnic background (i.e., diffused or foreclosed identities). White students, in particular, may show little interest in their ethnicity because they do not see themselves as having an ethnic background. However, it is just as important for White adolescents to examine their Whiteness as an identity and cultural system. Proweller (1999) stated, "the conflicts that White students experience when asked to talk openly about Whiteness as a location of racial identity reflect a profound resistance to examining their own positionality, lived experience, and racial histories of domination and oppression" (p. 808). Proweller further indicated that many White students do not avoid active engagement with race but selectively engage in "race talk" within the parameters of a polite and public discourse. For this reason, school counselors should provide "safe but challenging" environments for White students to openly discuss their racial identity and beliefs about race relations in this country. Safe environments include settings in which students are expected to respect one another, different opinions are valued and challenged, and students are open about their own identity development.

Counseling Snapshot

J'Nita, an African American eighth grader, is an honors student at Frederick Douglass Middle School. Because J'Nita is a student leader and has scored extremely well on gifted and talented tests, she has been selected to attend a special 3-week gifted and talented summer camp. J'Nita is not excited and has told her counselor that she does not want to go. She is concerned about what the other girls (who are African American) will say about her going to a camp for 3 weeks with "a bunch of White girls." She would rather stay home and "hang out" with her Black friends.

What would you, the school counselor, say to J'Nita? How does J'Nita's dilemma relate to her ethnic identity? What would be a "good" solution for J'Nita's problem?

Offering Diverse and Representative Resources

Considering the importance of ethnicity in the identity development of students, school counselors should examine counseling resources for cultural sensitivity and appropriateness. For instance, implementing bibliotherapy (i.e., therapy using books with characters experiencing a circumstance similar to the student in counseling) with books that include only White characters reinforces a lack of ethnic exploration and acceptance. School counseling offices should, therefore, offer books, videos, and other resources with representation of people-of-color and various cultures

Ethnic Identity Questions for Adolescents

Below are prompts that can be used in a small group with students. Counselors should respond to these items as well.

I consider myself to be _____ (enter ethnic group).

My ethnic group membership means _____.

I feel _____about my cultural or ethnic group.

I am happy to be a member of the group I belong to because

_____.

I am not happy to be a member of my cultural or ethnic group because _____.

Because I am _____, I am treated _____

_____.

to promote students' exploration and acceptance of their ethnic heritages. Also, school counselors should provide opportunities for positive acknowledgment of students' ethnic group membership in classroom guidance lessons, small groups, and any other school counseling activity. See the following ethnic identity questions that can be used in small groups.

The ethnic identity development of students is often influenced by the racial identity development of teachers and educators that they interact with at school. Helms (1990) describes positive White racial identity as involving the abandonment of racism and the development of a nonracist White identity. She outlines six ego schemas (formerly known as stages or statuses) in her model: Contact, Disintegration, Reintegration, Pseudo-Independence, Immersion/Emersion, and Autonomy. The *contact* schema is characterized by a lack of awareness of cultural and institutional racism, fear of people-of-color based on stereotypes, and lack of understanding White privilege. Individuals in this stage have identities that are based on perceptions of their personal traits and their adoption of beliefs espoused by family and social group members. School counselors in this schema are likely not to perceive cultural differences and oppression among students, because they "do not see color" and have little awareness of diverse people.

The *disintegration* schema begins when the White individual has a new understanding of cultural and institutional racism. The individual may experience guilt, shame, and sometime anger at the recognition of one's own advantage because of being White (i.e., White privilege). Whites in this schema become conflicted over racial moral dilemmas that are frequently perceived as opposites. For instance, a counselor may believe she is non-racist, yet she refuses to acknowledge racist practices at her school. School counselors in this stage may attempt to develop cross-ethnic relationships with students and colleagues, but these relationships are likely to be superficial (Marshall, 2002). Also, school counselors in this stage may experience dissonance and conflict between choosing between own-group loyalty and challenging oppressive practices in schools.

The next schema, *reintegration,* is characterized by the White individual regressing or reverting back to a dominant ideology associated with race and one's own socioracial group identity. There is a firmer and more conscious belief in White racial superiority, and racial-ethnic minorities are blamed for their own problems. A school counselor in both disintegration and reintegration statuses, will acknowledge differences in their students but fail to institute new practices and challenge policies that hinder the success of marginalized and oppressed youth. School counselors in the reintegration status will tend to be angry about professional development or training related to diversity because they believe that they have no role in remedying oppression or the problems of ethnic or cultural minorities.

A person is likely to move into the *pseudo-independence* schema after a painful or insightful encounter or event occurs that moves the person from the reintegration schema. In this schema, the person attempts to understand cultural differences and may reach out to interact with culturally different persons. However, the choice of culturally different persons is based on how "similar" they are to him or her. Persons in this schema tend to conceptualize racial and cultural issues in an intellectual manner. School counselors in this schema, may reach out to culturally different colleagues but not to culturally diverse parents or others outside of the school setting. Pseudo-independent counselors understand White privilege and the sociopolitical aspects of race and issues of prejudice and oppression but their understanding is from an intellectual perspective only.

The *immersion/emersion* schema is characterized by the White individual engaging in self-exploration as a racist being. The person becomes more aware of what it means to be White and how he or she benefits from White privilege. There is a willingness to confront one's own biases, and to become more of an activist in combating racism and oppression. The school counselor in the immersion/emersion schema is ready for a social justice approach to school counseling. He or she is able to recognize oppressive practices in schools, is willing to confront and challenge overt and covert racist actions, and is honest about his or her own biases and White privilege.

And finally, the *autonomy* schema involves the White individual's increased awareness of his or her own Whiteness, reduced feelings of guilt, acceptance of one's own role in perpetuating racism, and a renewed determination to abandon White entitlement. A school counselor in this schema is knowledgeable about racial, ethnic, and cultural differences, values diversity, and is not fearful, intimidated, or uncomfortable with the reality of race. The final list in the Suggested Readings section at the end of the book offers a short selection of titles that will help counselors understand and address issues of racial and ethnic identity development.

ASSESSING SCHOOL COUNSELORS' MULTICULTURAL COUNSELING COMPETENCE

Perhaps one of the greatest challenges confronting the social justice–focused school counselor is acquiring multicultural counseling competence. According to Ponterotto and Casas (1987), multicultural competence is achieved when a counselor possesses the necessary skills to work effectively with clients from various cultural backgrounds. Hence, a counselor with high multicultural competence acknowledges client-counselor cultural differences and similarities as significant to the counseling process. On the other hand, a counselor with low multicultural competence provides counseling services with little or no regard for the counselor's or client's culture and/or ethnicity.

Over the past three decades, the literature regarding multicultural counseling competence has focused on three main areas or dimensions: awareness, knowledge, and skills (Sue, Arredondo, & McDavis, 1992). The first area, *awareness*, stresses the counselor's understanding of their own personal worldviews and how they are the products of their own cultural conditioning. The second area, *knowledge*, reinforces the importance of counselors having an understanding of their clients' worldviews. Sue and colleagues (1992) pointed out that counselors must understand as well as respect their clients' worldviews. Traditionally, counseling, like other disciplines, has accepted culturally different persons if they were willing to become acculturated and reject cultural distinctiveness. This "melting pot" philosophy creates negative consequences if counseling techniques designed for the dominant culture are used inappropriately with clients of ethnically dissimilar backgrounds.

Finally, the *skills* area covers the counselor's ability to use culturally appropriate intervention strategies. Counseling effectiveness is improved when counselors use techniques and interventions that are consistent with the life experiences and cultural values of their clients.

In addition to the three-dimensional framework of multicultural competence, other perspectives regarding multicultural competence have been offered. Holcomb-McCoy and Myers (1999) suggested that there could possibly be more than three dimensions to multicultural competence. They proposed that one must also have knowledge of multicultural terminology and racial identity development theories. Pope-Davis, Reynolds, Dings, and Ottavi (1994) suggested that multicultural competence in counseling is "an appreciation of and sensitivity to the history, current needs, strengths, and resources of communities and individuals who historically have been underserved and underrepresented by psychologists" (p. 466).

Perhaps one of the first steps to becoming a multiculturally competent school counselor is to determine the knowledge and skill areas that one needs to develop or improve. The School Counselor Multicultural Competence Checklist (Resource B at the end of the book) can be used by professional school counselors to determine areas for additional multicultural counseling training. Based on the Association for Multicultural Counseling and Development's Multicultural Competencies and Explanatory Statements and multicultural education literature, the checklist encompasses competencies that have been noted as important for culturally competent work in school settings.

THE INFLUENCE OF CULTURE ON INTERVENTION PLANNING

As stated previously, there is a critical need for social justice–focused school counselors who are able to take culture into account when assessing and planning interventions for students. Culture determines, to a large extent, how a student experiences, identifies, interprets, and communicates a problem in school. At the same time, counselors' cultural misunderstandings or reliance on stereotypes can lead to faulty conceptualizations and interventions. School counselors need to be able to differentiate between the nuances of normal and dysfunctional patterns. This section of the chapter describes important components of culturally appropriate problem assessment and intervention planning.

1. Determining the Problem

It is the school counselor's responsibility to gather sufficient information about the student's presenting problem, and then be able to negotiate with the student the appropriate intervention. The school counselor's first task is to clarify from the student's perspective the nature of the problem that brings the student in for help. Ideally, the counselor is aware that it is inappropriate in some cultures, particularly for strangers, to ask personal questions. The school counselor should also keep in mind that some items of necessary information may have special cultural meaning. For instance, some cultures view talking directly and frankly to parents as disrespectful.

Reasons for Referral

In addition, the counselor should inquire about the immediate reasons for the referral as well as the specific situations of the complaints. Differences in opinion on the part of parents, caregivers, teachers, and other referral sources, and the child about the severity or frequency of a behavior should be identified. Misunderstandings about the reason for the referral should be addressed with the student and the individual who referred the student. An evaluation of a student who may be viewed as "culturally different" requires the counselor to explore possible cultural influences that may have precipitated the referral. The following vignette is illustrative.

> Sam, a 10-year-old African American boy, was referred to the counselor for disrespectful behavior in the classroom. Described by his teacher as confrontational, aggressive and too autonomous, Sam demanded more freedom and challenged his teacher on classroom rules and practices. His parents' childrearing had promoted assertiveness and independence.
>
> The differences in Sam's parents' and teacher's perceptions of Sam were clear. His teacher perceived him as an aggressive and "bad" young man. She regarded his behavior as a possible indication of an emotional disturbance or deviance. Sam's parents, on the other hand, viewed his behavior as a sign of strength and as that of an independent young man.
>
> The school counselor learned that Sam's parents sent him to a progressive, Afrocentric school to achieve their goal of a good, multicultural education for their son. At that school, Sam had been told to speak up, know his mind, question authority, and to be independent. The school counselor arranged a meeting between the teacher and the parents to clarify the mixed messages given to Sam. After a series of meetings directed by the school counselor, the teacher became more aware of the family's cultural beliefs and values and helped Sam integrate both philosophies.

The Contexts of Environment and Family

Details on the duration and degree of a student's problem should be explored within the context of his or her environment. Chronological details of the problem behavior, from the onset of the first symptoms to the characteristics of the presenting problem, should be identified and recorded. The school counselor should try to determine the extent to which the behavior is reactive to recent events in the child's environment. For instance, a student is referred to the school counselor for excessive fighting. The counselor examines the cumulative folder and realizes that the student has no past history of fighting and that his excessive fighting started 2 months ago. The counselor discovers that the student's family recently moved into a hotel because they are homeless. The counselor realizes that the fighting is a reaction to the recent stress of moving and being homeless.

It is critical to make determinations about students' behaviors in the context of their family's culture and to examine its meaning to the child and the community. Information should be gathered about any previous counseling or mental health treatment for the presenting problem (e.g., the frequency of sessions, the length of treatment, and the child's and family's response to treatment). If no formal treatment was sought or provided, the school counselor should inquire whether the family approached others within the community for help—for example, religious leaders, community leaders, godparents, or healers. This type of information provides a good sense of the family's help-seeking behavior and their previous experience in resolving their problems.

2. Developmental History

Obtaining a student's developmental history is an important component in determining the most appropriate intervention. The school counselor's goal in obtaining developmental history is to review behavioral patterns of childhood. When discussing the pregnancy and delivery of the child, the counselor must inquire about the parents' sociocultural attitudes about pregnancy, motherhood, and fatherhood, and then evaluate the influence of those attitudes on the development of their child. Data should be obtained about any special diets, medications, feelings about prenatal health care, as well as cultural attitudes in regard to diet and food cravings. Sample questions might include:

1. Who in the immediate community supported and advised the mother about ways to ensure a safe pregnancy?

2. Did the mother/father understand the risks of smoking and taking drugs or alcohol before and during pregnancy?

3. Was the child's father available and supportive, and if not, who was available to provide support?

4. Was the mother exposed to any stressful life events during the pregnancy?

5. Were there any complications in the delivery?

Despite its sensitive nature, there is a need to ask about previous infant losses. The counselor can then address the impact of such losses on maternal and paternal attitudes toward other children. School counselors should also determine whether the parents had a preference for the sex of the baby, how the baby's name was selected, what process was followed in naming the child, and whether the mother experienced any period of post-partum depression. Cultural attitudes toward weaning practice, physical arrangements in the household, decisions about the primary caregiver and feeding should all be discussed when assessing students' problems. The importance of eliciting a student's early developmental history is demonstrated in the following example:

> Victor, a 6-year-old Central American child, was referred to the school counselor with school phobia and immature behavior. When the school counselor talked to his parents, it was learned that the child still slept with his parents and was not yet weaned from the mother's breast.
>
> The parents informed the school counselor that in their culture the decision to leave the parental bed was always made by the child. After further questioning, it was learned that the older children in the family had made this decision at a much earlier age.
>
> Prior to Victor's birth, the mother lost two infant children. When the parents first arrived in this country, the parents were still mourning and Victor was born not long after their arrival.

3. Child Behavior and Development

Expectations concerning children's development and behavior vary across cultures and therefore must be assessed in a culturally sensitive manner. Attributes such as passivity, dependence, and the acquisition of language and motor skills have different meanings and symbolism in different cultures. For instance, one culture may tolerate delayed motor development but not delayed verbal acquisition. In some cultures, a child with learning difficulties may be shown more tolerance than a child who demonstrates anxious behavior.

Language and communication must be assessed within a student's cultural community. Some cultures highly value and reinforce early verbalization and fluency. Others show primary concern about early socialization skills and affective expression. School counselors should also pay special attention to a family's view of bilingualism.

4. Childrearing Practices

The school counselor needs to frame child-rearing practices within the context of a student's immediate home environment and the child's stage of development. It is particularly important to compare and contrast a family's attitudes with those of the community and larger society. Counselors should pay close attention to a student's views on sex and gender-role expectations because views about sexual education and sex role behavior vary among cultures. Some cultures and families use humor and short stories to teach their children about sexuality whereas others teach nothing about sexuality. Some cultural groups grant men greater and earlier independence than women.

For a student whose family immigrated to the United States gender expectations in a student's home culture may differ significantly from those in the new culture. A change in gender role as a result of immigration creates considerable conflict in some families. It is also important to understand the particular role of gender and age in a student's culture. For example, the firstborn son may be expected to assume tremendous responsibilities, regardless of his age, if the father is absent.

The school counselor should also assess a family's attitudes toward authority and their ability to determine an adequate punishment for rule infractions. Cultures vary in their styles of discipline, which may involve physical punishment, embarrassment or shame, withdrawal of love, suspension of social and recreational activities, or deprivation of toys and other forms of entertainment. Physical punishment has become a highly charged issue in communities where physical abuse is prevalent and has to be reported. The school counselor must be able to assess when the cultural norm of physical punishment becomes abusive and dangerous and must help parents find alternative and effective approaches that are culturally sensitive. Furthermore, in some cultures families may use disciplinary styles that are inconsistent. For example, boys are punished differently than girls and adolescents differently than elementary children.

5. Role of Extended Family

For many culturally diverse groups, an extended family functions as a source of support and as a means by which cultural and religious values are communicated. For instance, for many Latino subcultures (e.g., Mexican Americans), the family structure is characterized by formalized kinship relations to the godparent system and by loyalty to the family. Often, the extended family takes priority over other social institutions. Native American families include parents, children, aunts, uncles, cousins, and grandparents in an active kinship system. And, the extended family in African American culture is quite significant. Boyd-Franklin (1989) states, "Many Black families function as extended families in which relatives with a variety of blood ties have been absorbed into a coherent network of mutual emotional and economic support" (p. 43). An assessment of extended families might arise in cases like the following.

> JaVonte Simpson, a 12-year-old student, was referred to the school counselor for fighting at recess. When the counselor met with JaVonte's parents, she discovered that the family was living with Mrs. Simpson's mother (Ms. Brown) and her two youngest children (ages 24 and 25). Mr. and Mrs. Simpson's were forced to move JaVonte and his younger sister to Ms. Brown's house after a fire destroyed their apartment. Ms. Brown's apartment has two bedrooms, a living room, a kitchen, and a bathroom. Mr. and Mrs. Simpson were given the smallest bedroom, which they share with JaVonte and his sister. Ms. Brown's youngest children sleep in the living room.
>
> Both Mr. and Mrs. Simpson described the living arrangement as a nightmare. They discussed how they couldn't discipline their children or raise them in terms of their own lifestyle. JaVonte, his sister, and Ms. Brown's children are furious at each other because of the disruption in their lives.

Questioning the student about the structure of their family and asking them to identify those members with whom they get along best and least is a good way to obtain information about a student's extended family. After drawing a picture of the family, counselors may ask students to indicate the family member they love, fear, and dislike most, as well as the one they worry about most and the one they fight with most frequently. Counselors may ask similar questions about peers and teachers.

6. School History

Once a counselor has gained the trust of the student and the student's family, he or she should gather information regarding the student's school history. A school history should include a list of the different schools that the child has attended, attendance rates at each, and reasons for each school change. Many culturally diverse students may be kept out of school to help parents in the home or to serve as translators between their parents and government agencies. Other reasons for missing school can be extended visits to their country of origin, skipping school, or babysitting younger siblings. School counselors need to address the following when assessing a student's school history:

1. student achievements;

2. grade failures;

3. special class placements;

4. attendance at boarding schools, private schools, and so forth;

5. disciplinary actions;

6. presence of school phobias; and

7. history of truancy.

The student should be asked which teachers, subjects and classmates he or she likes most and least. If the student has attended several schools, the school counselor can ask about the school the child liked the best (and least) and why. The student's answers to questions about his or her participation in and reaction to extracurricular activities, bilingual programs, and enrichment programs should be noted. The student might also be questioned about any experiences that singled him out for ridicule or praise.

7. Insight, Judgment, and Coping Skills

The school counselor should also address a student's understanding of the reasons for the referral and the basis of his or her problem and how it might be corrected. To elicit information about the child's insight, judgment, and coping skills, the counselor might select one of the hypothetical scenarios that follows.

Scenario 1: You are the only African American in your class. Your classmates tease you and call you dumb. How would you feel? What would you do?

Scenario 2: A 16-year-old girl and family emigrated from Thailand a year ago. The girl now wants to be identified as a typical American girl, but her parents object to her dating outside of her ethnic group. They are angry about her disregard for the customs of their homeland. If you were this girl, what would you do?

Scenario 3: Seventeen-year-old Bryan, the oldest of five children, has grown afraid to go to school because of the gay bashing and hate crimes in his neighborhood and school. Bryan is gay and has been physically threatened by several heterosexual students. What would you do if you were Bryan?

QUESTIONS TO CONSIDER

1. List three counseling strategies or methods that you use frequently with students. Are the strategies culturally sensitive? Is there research to support their use with students of varying backgrounds?

2. Describe a time when you felt empowered to make a change or to demand a change. What did you do? What skills did you use? With colleagues, discuss how you can use your experiences to help a student or a parent feel more empowered.

3. How would you respond to a difficult student who claims that you "don't care, you are just like the other people in this school"? What will you say? What will you do to retain the student's trust and confidence? How would you approach a difficult parent who has the same claims?

4 Consultation

The greatest distance between people is not space. The greatest distance between people is culture.

—Jamake Highwater (Native American choreographer, author, and lecturer)

Consultation is a very powerful process that is indirect in its approach, but has the capacity to affect large numbers of students. I believe that social justice–focused school counselors should spend a significant amount of time working as school-based consultants. For it is in this role that school counselors can work to change or alter teachers', parents', or other educators' faulty thoughts and beliefs about students. It is also through consultation that school based consultants can train school personnel to implement innovative and creative approaches to working with students. This chapter offers a short overview of what consultation is, the impact of culture on consultation, and how consultation can be used as a means to advocate for better student and family services. The chapter ends with an introduction to school culture and its impact on the consultation process.

DEFINING CONSULTATION

Consultation has been defined as "a method of providing preventively oriented psychological and educational services in which consultants and consultees form cooperative partnerships and engage in a reciprocal, systematic problem-solving process to enhance and empower consultees, thereby promoting students' well-being and performance" (Zins & Erchul, 2002, p. 625). Consultation has three participants: the consultant, the consultee, and the

client or problem (see Figure 4.1). The consultants are the skilled professionals that have an understanding of both the consultation process and the
consultees and their problems. The consultee typically brings the problem
to the consultant and initiates the consultation process. Consultees are
often teachers, parents, or administrators. The client is typically a student or
a problem related to a particular student or group of students, parents, or
teachers. In schools, consultation involves adults (e.g., consultant-teacher,
consultant-parent) attempting to change or alter a student problem. The
client or student is not directly involved in consultation.

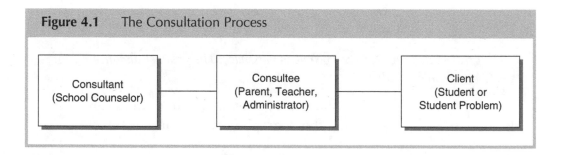

Figure 4.1   The Consultation Process

School-Based Consultation

School-based consultation that is social justice–focused and culturally
sensitive involves a consultant who adjusts his or her services to address the
needs and cultural values of the consultee, the client, or both. School counselors as consultants working from a social justice framework understand
the culture of schools and schools as a system. Counselor-consultants understand that policies and norms within the system have a direct influence on
the quality and types of services provided to students. Social justice–focused
consultants challenge unjust practices and degrading policies, and they
advocate for high expectations and success for students and their families.

Diversity Issues

Counselors will undoubtedly encounter issues related to diversity when
consulting with parents and teachers. However, in existing research and
training, the potential for understanding multicultural issues in consultation has received limited attention. Most of the literature written on multicultural issues in consultation has been published in school psychology
journals and books, whereas virtually no discussion of multicultural consultation has been found in the school counseling literature. Clearly, when

consulting with educators and parents, consultants need to understand the power of environmental and societal factors on the client (e.g., child), the consultee, and the consultation process.

SOCIAL JUSTICE CONSIDERATIONS AND THE CONSULTATION PROCESS

In the classic multicultural consultation article, Gibbs (1985) suggested that the culturally skilled consultant should not be "color blind." Although the intent of colorblindness may be to remove bias from the process, it can serve to deny the existence of differences in students' and consultees' perceptions of society arising from membership in culturally diverse groups. Overall, school-based consultants are ineffective if they ignore the influence of culture on their behavior, their consultee's behavior, and their client's behavior.

Cultural Differences

Cultural differences have been found to be significant factors in the counseling relationship, including difficulties establishing trust and rapport. The same has been purported to be the case in consultation. For instance, Gibbs (1985) indicated that African American teachers responded differently to outside consultants than White teachers. She found that White teachers were quicker to trust a consultant and embrace the goals of consultation. African American teachers, on the other hand, were more interested in building a relationship of trust with the consultant. Gibbs purported that African American consultees (i.e., teachers) preferred an interpersonal rather than an instrumental consultant style. As a result of her observations, Gibbs recommended that consultants who work with African American consultees or teachers would fair better if they focused on relationship-building before the problem-at-hand. The research on Gibbs' model, nevertheless, has been contradictory. Duncan and Pryzwansky (1993), for instance, found that African American teachers in their study preferred the instrumental rather than the interpersonal style of consultation.

It is important to remember that school-based consultants should avoid blaming cultural differences as "the problem" (e.g., blaming a student's immigration status as the reason for a student's misbehavior). When cultural factors are viewed as the problem, the participants in consultation are more likely to feel powerless in the problem-solving stage. Therefore, demographic variables such as race, class, religion, or marital status of parent should never be perceived as the source of a student's or parent's problem. The following vignette provides an example:

> Sean, an 11-year-old White sixth grader, has been referred to the counselor because of his lying and behavior problems in class. Ms. Rogers, Sean's mother, is single with four children, ages 17, 16, 11, and 7. The counselor decides to consult with Ms. Rogers about Sean's problem behavior. After discovering that Ms. Rogers is single, the counselor assumes that Sean's problems stem from his mother's marital status. "If Sean had a father in the home, he would be better behaved." The problem, according to the counselor, is the mother's marital status rather than what is happening in Sean's classroom.

The counselor in the above vignette made a mistake by blaming Sean's problem on a cultural difference or a demographic characteristic (e.g., marital status of mother). It is quite possible that Sean's problem behavior is related to Sean's feelings about school or classwork, his peer relationships, or the teacher's classroom management. The counselor should gather more information about Sean's behaviors and feelings before making a conclusion.

CONSULTATION STRATEGIES

The strategies used in consultation can be roughly divided into two types: those that focus on the presentation of new information or ideas as the primary change agent and those that focus on the relationship between the consultee and the consultant as the source of change.

The Problem With Presenting Only Information

Many consultants view the consultant–consultee relationship as important only to the extent that it facilitates the dissemination of knowledge regarding appropriate parenting and teaching practices. Such consultants generally adhere to behavioral or cognitive-behavioral theories and use psychoeducational approaches to alter student behavior. This approach can create several problems if cultural factors are not taken into account. Parents from historically oppressed and culturally diverse backgrounds may be suspicious of behavior modification techniques that use terminology such as *aversive conditioning, behavior control, extinction,* and *stimulus-reward.* For many parents, these terms infer intrusive treatments and possibly damaging interventions.

Consultation based solely on education and imparting information may also fail to consider the importance of psychosocial influences such as family structure, cultural value systems, interactional patterns, and adaptive coping strategies on behavior and functioning in culturally diverse families. For example, Latino, Hispanic, and Asian American families traditionally involve extended families such as grandparents to a greater extent in family decision making and child-rearing practices.

In addition to differences in family structure, consultation may be influenced by the adaptive coping strategies of many culturally diverse groups. These coping strategies (e.g., suspicion of outsiders, group unity) are necessary to deal with hostile environments and are often misdiagnosed as pathological if not examined within the appropriate cultural context. There is literature documenting the misclassification of African American and Hispanic children as having behavior problems (Oswald, Coutinho, Best, & Singh, 1999).

Consultants who work with parents should be cautious in assuming that referred Hispanic and African American children have been accurately labeled or diagnosed. A consultant's attempts to change what are assumed to be maladaptive behaviors may lead to ineffective interventions not addressing the true source of difficulty or, most important, to resistance and hostility from parents. The child in the following vignette provides an example:

Anthony Hill, a 5-year-old African American kindergartner, was brought to the counselor because of his biting, hitting, and screaming episodes in class. Because his behaviors disrupted class, he was sent to the principal's office for at least an hour per day. After many attempts to change Anthony's behavior through contracts and punishments, the child study team gives Anthony a nonclassified disability label. As a follow-up, the child study team recommended that the counselor consult with Ms. Hill (Anthony's mother) about ways in which to discipline him at home. The counselor-consultant met with Ms. Hill and discovered that she had very little knowledge of discipline strategies or parenting techniques. The counselor also discovered that Ms. Hill has set no rules or boundaries for Anthony and that he gets very little sleep because he stays up watching TV until 1 or 2 o'clock in the morning. The counselor realized that Anthony may not have a disability; rather his behavior is the result of his mother's lack of parenting skills. The counselor advocates for Anthony to be reevaluated so that he is not inappropriately labeled as "emotionally disturbed."

The Benefits of Developing the Relationship

Consultants working for social justice assume that the establishment of a warm and supportive relationship is a prerequisite to a significant change in the behavior of teachers or parents. Both consultants and consultees may enter into the consulting relationship with preconceived and inaccurate expectations of each other that are based on both conscious and unconscious perceptions. Asian cultures, for instance, traditionally view relationships to be hierarchical and value deference to authority figures. Parents adhering to such cultural values may, therefore, expect the consultant to provide advice and direction, whereas a parent with more Westernized values may expect more of an egalitarian relationship. African Americans have been reported to present passive resistance in helping alliances because of their anticipation of racial prejudice and discrimination by White American counselors. This resistance often leads to early termination and discontent with the services provided. In consultation with African Americans parents and teachers, it might be expected that they would display passive behavior, resistance, and early termination of consultation services (Locke, 1998).

The consultation relationship may also be influenced by the consultant's attitudes and beliefs. For example, Kalyanpur and Rao (1991) identified three qualities that were related to low-income African American mothers' negative perceptions of outreach consultants. First, *consultants' perceived lack of respect* for them and their *failure to trust them* were cited as significant barriers to fostering a collaborative relationship with the mothers. Second, the consultants' focus on the *mothers and their children's deficits* while ignoring their strengths also undermined the consultation relationship. The third factor leading to an impaired relationship between the mothers and the consultants involved a *lack of appreciation* toward the mothers' parenting styles, which were often blamed for children's behavior problems at school. In the following example, the counselor neglects to build on the parent's strength and positive attributes:

> Marian, an experienced school counselor, meets with Sharon, a single mother of two children at Marian's middle school. Marian is meeting with Sharon to discuss Sharon's oldest son, Trevor. Trevor is failing four out of his six classes. This is new behavior for Trevor; in the past, he maintained a "C" average in all of his courses. Marian starts the consultation session by stating, "Well, I'm glad you could finally come in. You were late the last time and I thought you were going to be late again." She then proceeds to tell Sharon what she perceives as the problem. "Well, Trevor is failing his courses and I believe you just need to discipline him more. Create a structured

study space for him and make sure he gets his work in. If you would give him structure, he would do better."

The Power of Advocacy

In many ways consultation can be regarded as a special form of advocacy that attempts to mediate and promote the actions of at least two other parties. For counselors in schools, consultation consists of going outside the counseling office and entering the classrooms and other elements of the school and community. For social justice–focused school counselors, consultation is often used as an advocacy tool. Advocating for the use of best teaching, learning, and parenting practices can have a powerful impact on student success.

A common consultation/advocacy scenario might involve a teacher who is having difficulties with a student with a behavioral or learning problem. The teacher, not trained in special education, is frustrated with the student's attitude and performance in class. The teacher tries a number of strategies and interventions and finds that nothing is working satisfactorily. In a school where consultation and advocacy are practiced, the counselor as consultant can provide the teacher with new information on behavioral techniques, get her assistance from experts in special education, and meet with her to develop modified classroom strategies and accommodations that better meet the needs of the student.

QUESTIONING DOMAINS

One of the most important aspects of consultation is the consultant's ability to ask the right questions to get the right information from the consultee. This process of questioning is critical because if the problem is misidentified then the interventions will not get to the root of the real problem. There are three domains of questions that should be addressed during consultation from a social justice perspective. Those domains are

- student domain,
- consultee (e.g., teacher, parent) domain, and
- environmental and cultural domain.

The student domain consists of questions regarding the student's characteristics, behaviors, and perceptions. Sample questions would include: What does the student do that concerns you? How is the student progressing academically? Does the student have friends? Describe the student's behavior in class. What are the student's strengths?

The consultee domain consists of questions regarding the consultee's behavior, skills, perceptions, and characteristics. Sample questions would include: What classroom interventions have you (the teacher) tried? What do you do when the student misbehaves? What do you like about the student? How might your beliefs and attitudes affect your response to the student?

The environmental and cultural domain consists of questions that cover cultural and environmental variables that could be influencing the problem. Sample questions include: What do the other students do when she misbehaves? What family issues might be influencing the student's problem? What classroom factors might be influencing the student's behavior? What role does the student's culture play in this problem?

Counseling Snapshot

Jim, a high school biology teacher, comes to you, the school counselor. Jim is having problems with a ninth-grade student who is openly gay. According to Jim, the student is belligerent, defiant, and talks too much in class. Jim tells the counselor that the student talks too much about his sexuality in class and that he annoys the other students. He says that he warned the student that he would send him to the office the next time he spoke out in class. The student has not changed his behavior and Jim wonders if he should have him taken out of his class.

Develop a list of questions that you would ask Jim, based on the three domains of consultant questions.

ASSESSING SCHOOL CULTURE

School-based consultants working from a social justice framework are very concerned about the school environment in which teachers, parents, and students must resolve their problems. For this reason, assessing a school's culture is critical component of school-based consultation. An assessment of a school's culture gives the consultant an idea of the context in which a problem is occurring and it helps the consultant determine how a problem can be resolved within a given environment.

The field of education lacks a clear and consistent definition of *school culture.* The term has been used synonymously with a variety of concepts, including *climate, ethos,* and *saga.* School culture involves the values, beliefs, and norms that lay the foundation for a school's climate, programs, and practices. School culture can also be defined as the historically transmitted patterns of meaning that include the norms, values, beliefs, ceremonies, rituals, traditions, and myths understood, maybe in varying degrees, by members of the school community. This system of meaning often shapes what people think and how they act. Unfortunately, one of the still prevalent underlying erroneous and harmful beliefs among both teachers and students is that children-of-color (e.g., African American, Latino or Hispanic, Native American, Asian American) come to school with cultural deficits. This belief is dangerous and translates into assumptions about what students can and cannot do. It is also often reflected in common educational practices, such as assigning African American students to special education classes at disproportionately higher levels. Thus, for many students-of-color, the school's negative perception of their ethnic group and culture creates a climate of low expectations and low performance that can evolve into self-degrading feelings and behaviors. To create schools that support high achievement of all students, school must transform their cultures in ways that result in the elimination of harmful institutional practices. Social justice–focused school counselors assess their school's culture and work to make it more positive and conducive to student success. More important, social justice–focused school counselors believe that school cultures can change.

Goldring (2002) divides school culture into three levels:

Level I: Things that can be observed. The way time and space is arranged, meetings are organized, budgets decided, communication and conflict managed, and celebrations held.

Level II: The values everyone believes in. Felt through behaviors and relationships of staff or symbols that represent the school.

Level III: Collected assumptions gathered by a group over time. These assumptions determine who is accepted in a group, the extent of sharing between members, and so forth.

Creating school cultures that help students become resilient is a critical aspect of school counseling in communities that are plagued by poverty, drugs, violence, poor nutrition, high mobility, and so forth. Resiliency is the ability to bounce back from persistent stress and crisis. Building caring support systems is one way in which resiliency is fostered and cultivated. Denbo (2002) indicated that schools that promote resilience have the following characteristics:

- promote close bonds
- value and encourage education
- use high-warmth, low-criticism style of interaction

- set and enforce clear boundaries (rules, norms, and laws)
- encourage supportive relationships with many caring others
- promote sharing of responsibilities, service to others, "required helpfulness"
- provide access to resources for meeting basic needs of housing, nutrition, employment, health care, and recreation
- set high and realistic expectations for success
- encourage goal setting and mastery
- encourage development of pro-social values (such as altruism) and life skills (such as cooperation)
- provide opportunities for leadership, decision making, and other meaningful ways to participate
- support the unique talents of each individual

SOURCE: Denbo, S. J., Institutional practices that support African American student achievement. In S. J. Denbo & L. M. Beaulieu (Eds.), *Improving schools for African American students*, copyright © 2002, pp. 56. Reprinted with permission from Charles C. Thomas Publisher.

Counselor in Action

What is the culture of your school? Think about your school's culture in terms of Goldring's three levels of school culture. List things that can be observed (e.g., rituals, ceremonies, celebrations, master schedules), important values that everyone believes in, and assumptions that are inherent in school policies, and so forth. What changes need to be made in your school's culture? Who determined the culture of your school?

Social justice–focused school counselors, teachers, and administrators can work together to promote these characteristics to create school cultures that nurture and promote resilience among students. As with good counseling, building resilience is rooted in developing meaningful and respectful relationships with students.

Social justice–focused school counselors are actively involved in the assessment of school culture. For more information on school culture assessment, school counselors can visit the following Web sites:

The Annenburg School Reform Institute: www.annenberginstitute .org/Tools/tools/results.php?fid=7

School Culture Net: www.schoolculture.net/index.html

See Resource C: School Culture Assessment for sample school culture assessment items.

QUESTIONS TO CONSIDER

1. How much time do you spend per week consulting with teachers? With parents? Is this more or less than what you desire? How much time do you believe you should be consulting? Why?

2. What are the three most prevalent issues or problems that bring teachers to you for help? What types of interventions or resolutions are used to resolve the problems? What would you like to do in the future to help teachers overcome these problems?

3. You determine that a teacher is biased against African American male students. How would you approach this topic with her? Role-play how you would discuss this topic in consultation.

5 Connecting Schools, Families, and Communities

Sustained unemployment not only denies parents the opportunity to meet the food, clothing, and shelter needs of their children but also denies them the sense of adequacy, belonging, and worth which being able to do so provides. This increases the likelihood of family problems and decreases the chances of many children to be adequately prepared for school.

—James P. Comer
U.S. psychiatrist and author

The key to increasing student achievement and ensuring more equitable practices in schools is to increase parent and community involvement. Although research has indicated for years that family involvement in schools increases student achievement, some schools are still slow to embrace real parent and community collaborations and partnerships.

Over the past decade, the participation of professional school counselors in the development and implementation of school-family-community (SFC) partnerships has also been endorsed and strongly encouraged in the literature (Bemak, 2000; Bryan & Holcomb-McCoy, 2004; Colbert, 1996). Most advocates for SFC partnerships believe that school counselors, if involved in SFC partnerships, may better meet the personal, social, academic, and career needs of larger numbers of students. In addition, it is believed that school counselors have the necessary skills (e.g., consultation, collaboration) to carry out the tasks related to promoting, developing, and implementing SFC partnerships

In school counseling programs that make social justice a priority, school counselors recognize the benefits of SFC and, therefore, spend a considerable amount of time working with parents and community-based organizations. They realize that with solid school-family-community partnerships, there will be higher test scores and grades, better attendance, more completion of homework, more positive attitudes and behavior among students (and parents!), higher graduation rates, and greater enrollment in higher education.

AVOID THE BLAME GAME

I have worked with many schools that have a culture of blaming and demeaning parents and communities. When working with an elementary school staff, I asked them to analyze data regarding parent participation in the parent-teacher organization, teacher conferences, and volunteering. The data showed that the same parents participated across all three parent activities. Essentially, only 2% of the parents in the entire school were actively involved in school-related activities and events. After examining parent data, we examined the amount of interaction between the school and its local community organizations, agencies, families, and so forth. There was only one community organization that was visible in the school and that was child protective services. It was apparent that the school staff had done very little to connect to the community it served. During our dialogue about the data, the following comments were made:

- The parents and community don't care about education because they don't come to the school! They only come to the school to complain . . .
- We've done all we can do to get more involvement!
- If only we had more parental involvement, then we could do our jobs better!

These types of statements shift the accountability away from the school professionals and onto the parents and community. Connecting schools, families and communities require that school professionals, parents, and community members share the responsibility of educating children. It also requires that educators and parents refrain from blaming one another for their challenges. They must collaborate and schools must develop policies that acknowledge the power of family involvement, activities that systematically infuse parents' and community members' perspectives and skills into school life, and ongoing evaluation to assess and improve the partnership. Three primary roles of the school include

1. giving parents access to information and skills to support their children's education,

2. coordinating community programming that meets the needs and issues that students and their families encounter, and

3. recognize the rights of parents—and their fundamental competence—to share in decision making.

This chapter provides guidelines for developing school-family-community partnerships by looking at the five principles of effective SFC partnerships as suggested by the Education Alliance at Brown University: policies, leadership, communication, community, and evaluation.

FIVE PRINCIPLES OF EFFECTIVE SFC PARTNERSHIPS

1. Policies

School communities rely on policies to guide their actions and inform their decisions. As such, specific policies regarding family involvement should be written to spell out the expectation that schools will institute, embrace, and support programs and activities that engage families and communities in children's education. Other critical policies (e.g., policies related to curriculum development, assessment, school climate) should be reviewed to integrate the parent perspective. Policies should reflect the attitude, mission, and philosophy of the school and its community. They should be developed collaboratively with parents to be certain they represent the concerns of families and foster family "ownership." See the example of an SFC policy below:

To support the mission of Mission Oaks Elementary School to educate all students effectively, schools and parents must work together as knowledgeable partners. The administration will support, through the California Department of Education, assistance in developing a strong comprehensive parent involvement program at Mission Oaks. The efforts should be designed to

- help parents develop parenting skills to meet the basic obligations of family life and foster conditions at home that emphasize the importance of education and learning.

- promote two-way (school-to-home and home-to-school) communication about school programs and students' progress.
- involve parents, with appropriate training, in instructional and support roles at the school and in other locations that help the school and students reach stated goals, objectives, and standards.
- provide parents with strategies and techniques for assisting their children with learning activities at home that support and extend the school's instructional program.
- involve parents in school decision making and develop their leadership skills in governance and advocacy.
- provide parents with skills to access community and support services that strengthen school programs, family practices, and student learning and development.

Thinking About . . . Your School

How does your school's mission statement demonstrate a commitment to family partnerships?

What family involvement policies currently exist in your school? What policies should be developed?

What other policies exist that should be reviewed and revised with family input?

How are parents, teachers, and community members involved in writing the policies?

How is information gathered from a wide range of parents to guide policy development (i.e., do you use surveys, interviews, etc.)?

How are parents involved in school leadership teams or councils? How could their roles be strengthened and improved? How are parents who typically don't participate involved? Are parent groups representative of all parents in the school's community?

Are family partnership policies resulting in higher achievement and a stronger school community? How is this assessed?

How do school policies reinforce state and district family involvement policies?

2. Leadership

School leadership has moved well beyond the authoritative model in which the principal and other school leaders make all the decisions. School counselors working from a social justice framework are leaders in the school, yet they understand that leadership must be shared with parents and the community to build a genuine sense of collaboration. Social justice–focused school counselors encourage and seek out the participation of nontraditional school leaders from families and the community. These nontraditional leaders would include clergy, small business owners, transportation workers, police officers, grandparents, uncles, aunts, godparents, and so forth.

For successful school-family-community partnerships, it is also important that an administrator or individual with "power and resources" assure that adequate funding exists to support school-family-community programs, space and equipment needs are met, that there is regular training and development for staff and community members, and the community is invited to play meaningful and appropriate roles in the school.

Thinking About . . . Leadership

What is your philosophy of leadership and what impact does it have on your school counseling program? Your work with parents?

Do you consider yourself a leader in your school? Why? Why not?

What is your principal's philosophy of leadership and what impact does it have on the school? On you?

What is your principal's view of how parents should be involved in the school and in their children's education?

How and when does your principal talk about family partnerships? Does he or she support teachers in discussing family partnerships regularly (e.g., at grade-level meetings)? Does the principal place expectations on teachers in that regard?

Does the school's budget include a line item supporting school-family-community partnerships?

Does the school have a staff member dedicated to coordinating family involvement? Is the school counselor involved in coordinating school-family-community involvement? Why or why not?

Are parents and community members involved in the planning, implementation, and evaluation of partnership activities?

Are parents and community members included at curriculum meetings, professional development workshops, and staff retreats?

---

3. Communication

Clear lines of communication build relationships between schools and families. Frequent, thoughtful, and diverse methods of communicating provide the strongest signals of genuine collaboration. Homes and schools hold critical information about children that must be shared. Families need to know what their children are learning and how to best support that learning at home. Teachers need to know about children's personalities, learning styles, and developmental history.

Families and schools should establish an expectation that communication will occur frequently and take many forms, including face-to-face meetings, regular written communications by e-mail, telephone, and special methods of contact when events warrant it. In addition to building pathways of information about children and their learning, schools should pay special attention to communicating in a culturally sensitive manner with clear and thorough information about the basics, such as school events, day-to-day logistics (e.g., child pick-up routines, the daily schedule, homework expectations), and how parents can access community support to support their parenting.

In addition to means of communication, schools should pay close attention to how educators communicate with parents. Giles (2005) contends that there are three basic narrative patterns underlying the relationships between parents and educators: (a) the Deficit (b) *In Loco Parentis*, and (c) Relational. In the *deficit* narrative, educators consider working-class and low-income parents to be deprived, deviant, or at-risk and have low expectations for their involvement in their children's education. The *in loco parentis* narrative shares the assumption that parents are not capable of contributing to their children's education and development but the educators assume that they can compensate for the parents' deficits themselves. In other words, there is a sense among educators that they can educate students in spite of their families, rather than in concert with them. And finally, there is the *relational narrative*. In this narrative, educators work *with* parents, rather than for them. Educators working within this narrative expect parents to bring knowledge and strengths to improving the school and parents expect educators to do the same.

Thinking About . . . Communicating With Parents and Families

How does your school communicate with parents and families? What is the rationale behind each method of communication? What are the gaps?

How well do teachers and other staff know their students' families?

How specifically does the school communicate with parents about learning and academics?

How are parents involved in decisions about their children's learning?

(Continued)

(Continued)

> How are parents greeted when they come into your school? Are parents of different cultural groups greeted differently? How quickly do they receive answers to their questions?
>
> How are families involved in suggesting and supporting home-school communications?
>
> How would the community, parents, and staff each describe the culture of your school?

4. The Community

Developing a school-family-community initiative targeting families-of-color and low-income families requires broad-based outreach with the help of representatives from all community stakeholder groups. Truly successful schools extend invitations to the community to participate and keep the community fully informed on school activities, progress, and performance. Participation can involve the sharing of experience from other contexts (commercial, service agency work), the exchange of ideas and information, connections to critical financial and material resources, valuable perspectives that can inform school mission and goals, and the reinforcement of the critical notion that the school and community are working toward common objectives.

Keeping the community fully informed about what is happening at the school leads to a sense of openness and honesty, illustrates the achievements of the school and the challenges that lie ahead, and builds support for annual budgets and new initiatives. A primary reason for schools to invest in creating community partnerships is to build the capacity of others to support the school and to nurture potential leaders.

In addition to working with community stakeholders, it is also important for social justice–focused counselors to identify the formal and informal power structures in the community, including the "top players" or most powerful community members, their connections, and their positions on education issues. Social justice–focused counselors should reach out to local politicians and state legislators with mailings and briefings about school-community initiatives. It is possible that they will support the initiatives for their own political gains. Here are sample selection criteria for SFC partnership committees.

Criteria for Selection of
School-Family-Community Committee Members

1. Identify and involve people whose support is absolutely critical, such as your school principal or chief administrator. If he or she does not actively support your initiative, it will never get off the ground. Also involve school faculty who will be directly affected by any changes in prevention programming. According to a national study, "activities that are initiated, selected, or planned by 'insiders' (i.e., persons within a school organization) tend to be more accepted by school staff; impulses to resist adoption or implementation sometimes triggered by programs imposed upon a school are less likely to be evoked" (Gottfredson et al., 2000).

2. Identify influential community leaders. These are people who can command attention, make decisions, involve others in positions of leadership, and provide access and influence. For example, a well-connected parent activist can rally a community around an issue.

3. Identify members from diverse backgrounds, including different religious, ethnic, age, and socioeconomic groups. If you have difficulty recruiting a diverse team, invite representatives from systems that represent or advocate for different groups.

4. Find people who have a strong interest in helping the school and community address problems. Passion and commitment will ultimately drive your initiative. Identify members who share your zeal and who will go the extra mile to get things done because they truly care about kids and believe in the potential of prevention.

5. Involve members whose positions, expertise, and skills match the purpose of your initiative. Initially, you may want to involve key stakeholders who can help you build community support. As your plan evolves and becomes more concrete, you will need to involve people who can help you implement your prevention strategies and, ultimately, institutionalize your efforts. For example:

1. If curriculum implementation is the focus of your work, make sure to involve teachers, curriculum coordinators, parents, nurses, and guidance counselors.

2. If changing community norms is your focus, involve grassroots activists and community citizens.

3. If service coordination is the focus, involve school counselors and psychologists, health care and social service providers, and teachers.

4. Involve students—and listen to them! Students know what's going on. They bring their own perspective on strategies that will be most effective and can help you get participation from the student body.

SOURCE: From *Promoting Prevention Through School-Community Partnerships*, U. S. Department of Education. (2006) Available online at http://www.ed.gov/admins/lead.saftey/training/partnerships/index.html

---

Thinking About . . . Community Partnerships

What partners has your school invited "to the table" to participate in essential school matters? Who is missing?

How does the school support community partners as they commit to supporting the school? How do each of the partners contribute? How do they benefit in return?

What technical support is needed to sustain partnerships (a meeting convener, regular e-mail updates, conference calls, etc.)?

How are nontraditional or harder-to-reach groups from the community contacted and involved?

Who are the nay-sayers in the community who could become better informed about the school and invited to participate?

How are the energies of different partners assessed? Are these partners being used to their best and most efficient advantage?

5. Evaluation

In a comprehensive and systematic way, the school should revisit goals, assess progress, and make adjustments in its family and community involvement programs. Evaluation efforts might focus on the satisfaction of the partners in terms of their roles, accomplishments resulting from family and community involvement (especially those relating directly to student achievement), lessons learned, and new elements to add.

Evaluation methods should be broad-based (including both qualitative and quantitative methods such as interviews, focus groups, and surveys), collecting information from the key players, as well as parents and community members in general. Although basic information can be helpful, such as the number of parents who attend meetings, it is also important to look deeply into important issues, such as how parent leaders have emerged and what strategies have worked to develop more diverse parent participation. Careful consideration should be given to how the original vision of family and community involvement has changed, what the new expectations are, and how programs and policies will support new directions.

Thinking About . . . Evaluation

What kind of evaluation has been conducted to assess the effectiveness of the family and community involvement program?

How thorough is the evaluation and what components could be added?

How are the lessons of evaluation used?

How are parents and community members involved in the evaluation design and implementation? How are they involved in the interpretation of results and the development of recommendations for change?

How do these changes specifically relate to student achievement?

BARRIERS TO SCHOOL-FAMILY COLLABORATIONS

Families have a variety of reasons for not becoming involved in schools , and those reasons should be considered before dismissing noninvolved parents as uncaring or uninterested. These obstacles can range from inconvenient meeting times to feeling unwelcome in the school. Social justice–focused school counselors are skilled and creative when planning SFC partnership activities and are aware of the obstacles that keep parents from participating and attending school events. The results from a national survey conducted by the Department of Education (2004) indicated that the percentage of students in kindergarten through grade 12 whose parents reported that they had acted as a volunteer at their children's schools or served on a school committee was higher for students in private schools (both church-related and nonreligious— 70% and 63%) than for students in public schools. The study further indicated that the percentage of students whose parents had attended a general school meeting was higher in households where parents had completed higher levels of education. Specifically, the percentage of students whose parents reported that they had attended a general school meeting was higher for children whose parents had attended graduate or professional school (95%) or completed college (92%) than for children whose parents had completed only a high school education or the equivalent (84%), and children whose parents had completed less than a high school education (70%). These results tell us that there is a clear gap between the involvement of parents according to SES and education level (see Table 5.1 on the following page).

Table 5.1 *Percentage of Elementary and Secondary Children Whose Parents Were Involved in School Activities by Parent and School Characteristics*

Parent and school characteristic	Attended a general school meeting	Attended a parent-teacher conference	Attended a class event	Volunteered at school
Race/ethnicity				
White	88.7	76.4	74.1	48.4
Black	88.7	78.7	63.3	32.0
Hispanic	82.6	78.1	60.9	27.7
Other	87.5	77.6	68.5	37.2
Education				
Less than high school	69.8	67.8	42.4	15.6
High school/GED	83.8	75.4	62.1	30.3
Vocational/ technical college or some college	88.5	78.0	69.1	38.8
Associate degree	88.6	76.6	73.0	39.7
Bachelor's degree	92.0	79.8	80.1	53.9
Graduate degree	94.6	79.4	80.8	61.8
Elementary school parent	96.6	91.6	88.4	73.4
Secondary school parent	93.0	72.2	77.6	55.2

SOURCE: From *Parent and Family Involvement in Education,* U.S. Department of Education, NCES, 2004.

Creative planning for overcoming relationship barriers with parents is essential to a social justice–focused school counseling program. School counselors should be well-equipped with ideas for connecting with hard-to-reach and untrusting parents. First and foremost, school counselors working from a social justice perspective should approach every meeting with a parent or community member with a positive attitude and welcoming disposition. Developing a strong working relationship with community members is the basis for SFC partnerships. For instance, starting a meeting with community members and parents with the following statement would not be appropriate, "OK, let's get started quickly because I have to be out of here by 4:00." Although the counselor really needs to leave by 4:00, making this the first statement sends a message to the group that the committee, including the parents and community members, is not very important. A better statement would have been, "I am so happy that we are getting this chance to meet. I know we have common goals and desires for the students at this school and I look forward to us working together. I have another meeting that starts after 4:00 and I must leave by then, but I want you to know that I am committed to working with you." Following are a few ways to overcome obstacles to parent attendance and participation in school activities, followed by a Counseling Snapshot.

Ideas for Overcoming Obstacles to Parent Attendance and Participation in School Activities

- Provide multiple times for parents to participate in school activities.
- Inform parents of a school event in multiple ways (e.g., send a "save the date" flyer, send personal letters inviting parents, send reminders written by students).
- Arrange car pools; provide bus or information about public transportation.
- Provide childcare.
- Arrange informal social event for parents and staff to become better acquainted.
- Conduct training for parents.
- Encourage parents to express their viewpoints.
- Consult with staff on ways to welcome parents.
- Do not discount anything that a parent says.
- Learn the cultural norms and customs of parents; then plan school events accordingly.
- Have clear goals and purpose for meetings.

Counseling Snapshot

Ms. Brown is a seventh-grade counselor at Riverdale Academy and she is the school liaison with the Family Resource Center (FRC). FRC is a community-based organization that provides services and support for Riverdale Academy's highly diverse student body and families. The school counselor works closely with the Family Resource Center and assists with the assessment of the community's needs. Being school-based, the FRC serves as a positive connection between families with diverse languages and the school staff. The FRC successfully communicates to families with diverse languages the importance of supporting their children's learning.

To increase communication with families, the FRC provides the following: a monthly roster of afterschool enrichment classes to decrease the number of children returning to an empty home after school, a library of books for parents on topics such as child development, self-enrichment classes for parents on topics such as CPR and school readiness, playgroups for parents and children not yet of school age, and other youth-development programs for parents and children. The FRC's afterschool activities provide critical support for families and contribute to improved student success. The FRC has successfully drawn families into the school community, while building strong relationships between the school and its families.

Although parents' barriers are often cited in the literature as the main reason for failed SFC partnerships, counselors and other educators are often resistant to developing closer relationships with parents and community members. Counselors will often state, "When do I have the time to create partnerships?" "My principal wants me to do other work, not partnerships!" or "I would if I had some help." Bryan (2005) recommends that counselors play the role of facilitator, advocate, and collaborator to increase SFC partnerships. She states that it is not enough to just build partnerships but school counselors must see their role in SFC partnerships as critical and integral to their school's ability to close achievement gaps. Resources to help school counselors strengthen SFC partnerships can be found online at the Web sites of the Center on School Family Community Partnerships (www.csos.jhu.edu/P2000/center.htm) and the Northwest Regional Educational Laboratory (www.nwrel.org/partnerships/links/index.html). The following examples highlight school counselors building SFC partnerships. To assess your beliefs about the role of counselors in SFC partnerships, see Resource D at the back of the book.

Counseling Snapshots

Mrs. Alvarez is the counselor at Avondale Elementary School, a school in a predominately low-income Latino inner city community. More than 3 years ago, Mrs. Alvarez initiated a meeting with various community organizations (e.g., churches, social service agencies, community activists, politicians) to discuss Avondale's low test scores, low attendance rates, and overall negative school culture. This was the type of initiative that would have alarmed most school officials; however, from this meeting, a committee (the Avondale Elementary School Community Organization) was formed to work and focus on school improvement.

The committee, with the help of Mrs. Alvarez and administrators, opened an after-hours community center in the school building that offered child care, adult literacy classes, GED classes, tutoring, parent services, and other needed resources. Mrs. Alvarez and her principal worked out an innovative school counselor schedule that allowed for Ms. Alvarez to work at the center on Wednesdays. Within 1 year, there was a 50% increase in test scores, more parents were volunteering to help in the school, teachers' morale had improved, and 42 residents had earned a GED.

---❖---

The School Counseling Department at Grand Hill High School developed a consortium with a local grassroots, community organization for the purpose of getting more parents involved in the education of their students. The grassroots organization, Parents Empowered, consists of community parents, school reform advocates, and community activists who want schools to respect and include parents in school change efforts. The school counselors attend the group's meetings and make reports regarding Grand Hill's student needs and issues. Also, the counselors act as consultants to the group regarding school improvement plans and school data. The principal at Grand Hill encouraged the counselors to collaborate with Parents Empowered because he believes that the school must support and validate parents' empowerment and organized efforts outside of school.

QUESTIONS TO CONSIDER

1. Describe recent efforts that your school has made to connect with parents and community members. How was the effort received? Describe.

2. What are some barriers that keep you from working on SFC partnerships? How can you overcome these barriers?

3. How do teachers in your school relate to parents? Walk around your school and make note of how school personnel talk to parents. How do school personnel talk differently to parents of different cultural groups?

6 Collecting and Using Data

It wasn't my love for numbers, but my passion for children that led me to study and use school and district data.

—Educator

I f I want to hear a gasp at a school counseling workshop or conference session, I only need to murmur the word "data." For some reason, when anyone brings up the word *data* at a school counselors' meeting, counselors become anxious. It is not uncommon to hear counselors say

- "I don't understand how to use data in school counseling . . ."
- "What data would I collect?"
- "What type of data do they want?"
- "Data doesn't measure what we do."
- "Where will we get this data?"
- "When will I have the time to collect and analyze data?"

Typically, I proceed with ease and try to calm counselors' fears and reassure them that we can do this! Eventually, we move beyond the fear of numbers to the ultimate goal of school change and effective practice. This is where social justice–focused counselors must be—at the point of using data for school change and school counseling reform. School counselors who are focused on social justice must use data to promote systemic and programmatic changes within schools and within counseling programs. If we want to close the achievement gap, then determining the effectiveness of our counseling programs and interventions must be a priority.

Although there are clear advantages to using data in schools, there are inappropriate uses of data too. Data should never be used as a tool for blame or to leverage personal or political gain. Data, in the most effective schools, are used to guide instruction, but never to exclude students from opportunities. For instance, using test scores (e.g., data) to determine which students should be excluded from special programs is not the best use of data, from a social justice perspective. Instead, data should be used to illustrate the limited access of gifted education to specific groups of students. In sum, data should be used primarily to validate the need for improvement, to monitor data-driven decisions, and to reveal inequities in access, attainment, and achievement within the school community.

WHAT IS ACCOUNTABILITY?

In this era of educational reform, greater emphasis is being placed on making school personnel accountable for bringing all students to high levels of academic performance. All school personnel and educational policymakers are responsible for establishing responsive policies and initiating new strategies to enhancing student success and learning. In addition to teachers and school administrators, ensuring the success of every student falls upon school counselors, too.

Webster's dictionary defines accountability as "the state of being accountable; liability to be called on to render an account; the obligation to bear the consequences for failure to perform as expected." The recent movement in education, more specifically the No Child Left Behind Act, focuses on the accountability of schools to students, parents, and communities. Parents and other community members are now able to access information regarding schools' educational progress. And, more important, if schools do not make progress, then parents are given other options to educate their children.

According to the American School Counselor Association's (ASCA) National Model, accountability is an important and integral component of a comprehensive school counseling program. The model requires counselors to demonstrate the effectiveness of their work in measurable terms such as impact over time, performance evaluation, and undertaking a program audit (Stone & Dahir, 2004). The goal of the National Model is for counselors to become more accountable to school and community stakeholders and to align their programs with standards-based reform. By using data to guide their programs and to illustrate effectiveness, school counselors become accountable to students, parents, communities, and their colleagues.

USING DATA TO UNCOVER INEQUITIES

Data can be useful in determining and uncovering inequities in schools. To detect inequities and unjust practices, school counselors must first consider important and critical questions regarding their programs or schools. What do I want to know about my school's ability to educate students? What questions do I have about my students? My school community? Asking difficult questions and developing a sense of inquiry is the first step to using data to promote social justice. Sample questions that might evolve include, "What percentage of each racial, ethnic, gender, and language group is reading at their grade level? What percentage of our students goes on to four-year colleges and universities? How many students are sent to the office daily from Ms. Lee's class? What is the breakdown of grade point averages by gender? By race? By ability?

Types of Data

Once the previous questions are developed, the counselors then need to gather the data to answer their questions. There are three types of data typically discussed in schools:

- achievement,
- attainment or access, and
- school culture data.

Achievement data includes PSAT, SAT, ACT, state tests, grades, and performance tests; *attainment* or *access data* includes promotion and retention rates, gifted and talented patterns, special education identification rates, postsecondary patterns, transition patterns, and enrollment patterns; and *school culture data* includes data regarding attendance, student-faculty relationships, student relationships, staff relationships, leadership styles, respect for diversity, suspensions and expulsions, dropout rates, and staff attitudes and behaviors.

Data can be either qualitative or quantitative. Quantitative methods are those that focus on numbers and frequencies rather than on meaning and experience. Quantitative methods (e.g., experiments, questionnaires, psychometric tests) provide information that is easy to analyze statistically.

Quantitative methods are associated with the scientific and experimental approach and are criticized for not providing an in-depth description. Qualitative data, on the other hand, is typically in the form of words, pictures, or objects. Researchers who desire qualitative data are concerned with describing meaning rather than with drawing statistical inferences. Qualitative methods for gathering data include interviewing people about their experiences, observing people, or gathering peoples' written descriptions of their experiences. For instance, Ms. Collins, an elementary counselor wanted to know more about students who were suspended and expelled. She decided that she needed school culture data regarding who was suspended in the past 6 months and she needed data regarding the number of reasons for the suspensions (quantitative data). In addition, she wanted to know the staff's and students' perceptions of the suspension policies (qualitative data). She then collected the names and grades of suspended students from the secretary (quantitative). She also retrieved the suspension forms, which included reasons for suspensions, from the Central Office (qualitative and quantitative). And finally, she interviewed and surveyed teachers, administrators, students, and parents regarding the school's suspension and expulsion policy (qualitative).

In many cases, school districts will have collected an abundance of data that a counselor can easily retrieve. School or district reports, accreditation reports, and information on Web sites contain data that a counselor might need to answer a particular question. If the data doesn't exist, counselors can generate their own data or can ask an individual within the district's research or accountability office for assistance. Whenever possible, counselors should collect at least two or three kinds of evidence or data to help answer a question. For instance, Ms. Collins in the previous example collected data from teachers, students, and she used existing data that was collected by her school and the district. Possible data elements include the following:

Grades	Gender
Standardized tests	Ethnicity
Graduation rates	Attendance
Retention rates	Discipline referrals
Enrollment in rigorous courses	Free-reduced lunch
Special education placement	Gifted and talented placement
Postsecondary enrollment	Enrollment in remedial courses

Analyzing Data

Whenever possible, data should be *disaggregated* by race, ethnicity, and gender to illuminate and analyze any inequities in student achievement, attainment, or access. If a school is racially and ethnically homogeneous, then data should still be disaggregated by cultural groupings (e.g., gender, socioeconomic status) and school/class characteristics (e.g., teacher, courses taken, grades). Table 6.1 shows data from an inner city high school in a predominately African American community. Although the data could not be disaggregated by ethnicity, gender is clearly a factor when discussing students' postsecondary aspirations. See Tables 6.1 and 6.2 for examples of disaggregated data.

Table 6.1 *College-Going Rate by Gender (Predominately African American School)*

Year	Males	Females	Number in Senior Class
2001	21	75	110
2002	15	68	100
2003	13	79	121
2004	12	85	119

Table 6.2 *School "X" Percentage of Suspensions by Ethnic Group, 2003–2006*

Suspensions	African American	Latino	White	Asian
2003	12	9	11	0
2004	10	6	6	0
2005	10	4	6	1
2006	8	4	4	0

To assist with the analysis of data, there are several statistical programs (e.g., SPSS, Excel) that can help with simple statistical procedures such as percentages and frequencies. One statistical program, EZAnalyze, was designed for school counselors and can be accessed on-line at www.umass.edu/schoolcounseling. Counselors should inquire about statistical resources within their own school districts because many districts have research personnel that are highly skilled statisticians and data analyzers.

Sharing Data

Tables, graphs, and pictographs (e.g., pie charts) are excellent ways to organize data for analysis, interpretation, and sharing. Some data may need to be represented in narratives, videos, or in their existing formats (e.g., course schedules, course syllabi). See Figure 6.1 for an example of a bar graph that communicates the number of suspensions in a school over a 3-year period, categorized by ethnicity. Data are typically shared with others by examining proportions of each subgroup represented in a particular group, curriculum area, program, test range, or so forth. For instance, a counselor may show data that reflect the number of students by ethnic group that are in a special magnet program. Also, data that reflect change or growth over time should be shared with others. A school counselor may, for instance, show data reflecting a math achievement gap between White and Latino students over a 3-year period.

When presenting data, counselors should be sure that the audience can understand the key points or highlights of the data. Data presentations should be easy to understand and the goals for presenting the data should be clear. Counselors must be ready to facilitate a dialogue about the data *and be willing to initiate discussions that are often taboo in the school setting. It is common (and a good thing!) for issues related to racism, discrimination, and bias to arise when examining achievement or attainment gaps.* Time and a safe environment should be provided for dialogue. Counselors should be prepared to encounter denial about what the data illustrate. Statements such as "Disaggregating data is racist" and "I understand the data, but that's just the way things are" are common "denial" statements that must be addressed in order to move forward.

Thinking About . . . Data Analysis

See Figure 6.2, which graphs placement patterns of special education students by racial and ethnic group over a 4-year period. What patterns or trends do you see? What contrasts are shown?

SCHOOL COUNSELING PROGRAM EVALUATION

Data can be used to evaluate school counseling programs and activities. School counselors can also use evaluation techniques to assess the extent to which stated goals and objectives are being achieved. Evaluation allows counselors to answer questions such as the following:

Figure 6.1 Percentage of school suspensions over a 3-year period, by ethnic group.

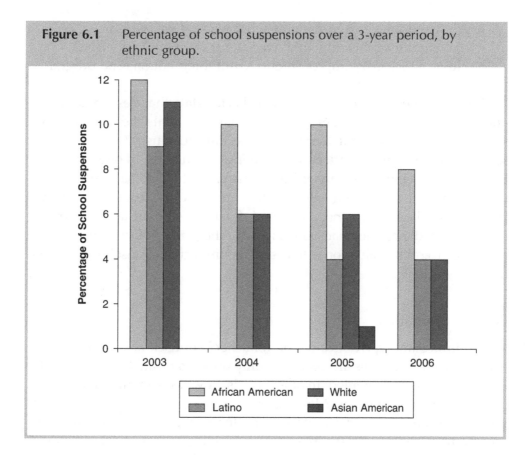

Figure 6.2 Percentage of students in special education, graphed by race.

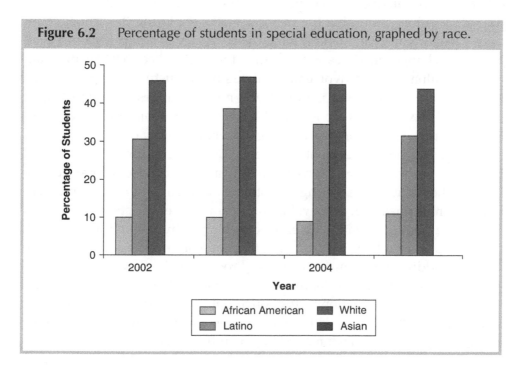

- Are we doing for our students what we said we would?
- Are students achieving what we set out for them to achieve?
- How can we make improvements to our interventions and programs?

For many years, school counselors collected data that described the frequency of counselor activities (e.g., how many students did the counselor see during a month?) but there was little data to illustrate what impact school counseling interventions were having on students. In one school district, the counselors were very efficient when asked to keep a record of how many groups they implemented or how many classrooms they visited. When asked how much those groups influenced student achievement or student attendance, they had no idea. Thus, the primary purpose of implementing program evaluation is to assess the impact of counseling interventions on students.

Process Evaluation

An important type of evaluation for school counselors is *process evaluation*. Process evaluations are geared to fully understanding how a particular intervention is implemented. In other words, how does an intervention produce the results that it does? Process evaluations are useful if school counselors have implemented an intervention for a long time, if students have seemed to lose interest in the intervention, or if the counselor would like for others to replicate the intervention. Process evaluation involves assessing the intervention, examining the methods used, exploring the school counselor's performance, and determining the adequacy of equipment and facilities. The changes made as a result of a total school counseling program process evaluation may involve immediate small adjustments (e.g., a change in how one particular unit is presented), minor changes in design (e.g., a change in how students are assigned to groups), or major design changes (e.g., dropping the use of a particular counseling activity or intervention).

In theory, process evaluation occurs on a continuous basis. At an informal level, whenever a counselor talks to another counselor or an administrator, they may be discussing adjustments to their program or interventions. More formally, process evaluation refers to a set of activities in which administrators or evaluators observe counseling activities and interact with counselors and students in order to define and communicate more effective ways of addressing counseling goals. Process evaluation can be distinguished from outcome evaluation on the basis of the primary evaluation emphasis. Process evaluation focuses on a continuing series of decisions concerning program improvements, whereas outcome evaluation focuses on the effects of a program on its intended target audience (i.e., the students).

SOARING

SOARING (Gilchrist, 2006) is an accountability and evaluation system especially designed for school counselors. The SOARING framework helps school counselors highlight the impact of counseling activities on students' achievement and/or behavior. The SOARING acronym stands for

S—Standards

O—Objectives

A—Assessment

R—Results

I—Impact

N—Network

G—Guide

SOURCE: From *School counselors are soaring in Virginia* [PowerPoint Presentation], by Dr. Sylinda Gilchrist, Copyright 2006. Reprinted with permission from Dr. Sylinda Gilchrist.

The first step in the SOARING approach is for school counselors to ask themselves what *standard* does the counseling activity address. At this point, the school counselor takes into account either the three domains of the American School Counselor Association's National Standards—academic, career, personal or social, or district or state standards. A counseling activity can address one or more standards. For instance, a college financial aid workshop is clearly in the career domain. However, the content of the workshop could include information that addresses academic and personal and social domain standards.

The next step of SOARING includes the development of *objectives* for the school counseling activity. The objectives should be measurable, speak to the purpose of the activity, and connect with the school's mission. For instance, an objective for a third-grade classroom guidance lesson on conflict resolution may state, "Third-grade students will be able to express two appropriate ways to resolve a given conflict after six classroom guidance lessons."

Next, the *assessment* phase of SOARING refers to the assessment of the objective. The important questions during this phase are "How will I determine whether I met my objective?" and "What type of data will I gather?" Possible data sources include grades, standardized test scores, attendance rates, discipline referrals, and pre- and posttests. Counselors can also use simple verbalizations from students that determine mastery of an objective.

For instance, a counselor might take note of how many students can verbalize two appropriate ways to resolve a conflict before a classroom guidance unit and then again after the conclusion of the unit.

The *results* phase of SOARING refers to gathering and calculating results from the assessment phase. The results should be clear and given in descriptive terms. Percentages and means are a great way to illustrate the impact of a counseling activity. Graphs and charts are also useful when explaining data results. As an example of calculating results, let's use the third-grade classroom guidance lesson pre- and posttest results. Before the series of classroom guidance lessons on conflict resolution, the counselor gave students a pretest including a question about how to resolve conflicts appropriately. Five of the thirty students (17%) stated two appropriate ways to resolve a given conflict. After the lessons, 20 of the 30 (67%) students could state at least two appropriate ways to resolve a conflict. This is a 50% increase (67%–17% = 50%).

After calculating results of an assessment, it is important to develop an *impact statement*. The impact statement describes the results and how the program affected students' achievement, attendance, behavior, and so forth. An impact statement might read as follows: "Third-grade students' knowledge of two ways to resolve conflict in an appropriate way increased from 5–30 after a conflict resolution unit (50% increase)."

The next phase, *network*, refers to the communication of results to important stakeholders (e.g., principals, superintendents, parents, teachers). The impact of counseling activities can be communicated via brochures, newsletters, or orally via reports to committees, community organizations meetings, and faculty meetings.

And finally, the *guide* phase includes a review of the results and decision about next steps. What worked and what did not work? What do I need to change? How can I extend this activity? In other words, the guide phase is a reflection period about what to do next. See Resource D at the end of the book for examples of SOARING worksheets.

Counseling Snapshot

Judy, an elementary school counselor, was planning to implement a 5-week study skills group for fifth graders. For the past 6 years, Judy has implemented 12 study skills groups using her 5-week group curriculum. In the past, students and teachers raved about her groups, but she had no data to illustrate that it was helping students study better and receive better grades.

After consultation with her supervisor about program evaluation, Judy decided to collect data related to her study skills group. Her overall objective for the students was, "As a result of participation in the study skills group, 90% of the students' grades will increase by one letter grade." A secondary goal of her group was "As a result of participation in the study skills group, 90% of the students' teachers will report that the students completed all of their homework during one semester." Judy collected the students' grades before and after the group to examine any grade change. She also developed a short questionnaire for teacher feedback on students' homework completion.

Counselor in Action

Choose one counseling activity that you love to do. What standards does the activity address? What are the objectives of the activity? Complete the SOARING worksheet on pages 139–140, based on your favorite activity. Develop an assessment tool to assess your objectives.

DEVELOPING PROGRAM ASSESSMENT TOOLS

Selecting the most appropriate means of determining whether students have achieved stated counseling objectives can take much thought. Traditionally, most assessments of students in the United States have been accomplished through the use of formalized tests. This practice has been criticized in recent years because such tests may not be accurate indicators of what the student has learned (e.g., a student may simply guess correctly on a multiple-choice item). Further, alternative approaches, which more fully involve the student in the evaluation process, have been praised for increasing student interest and motivation. This section looks at three assessment concepts: alternative assessment, performance assessment, and authentic assessment.

Standardized testing was initiated to enable schools to set clear, justifiable, and consistent standards for its students and teachers. Such tests are currently used for several purposes beyond that of classroom evaluation. They are used to place students in appropriate level courses; to guide students in making decisions about various courses of study; and to hold teachers, schools, and school districts accountable for their effectiveness based on their students' performance.

Alternative, Performance-Based Assessments

To encourage students to use higher-order cognitive skills and to evaluate students more comprehensively, several alternative assessments have been introduced. Generally, alternative assessments are nonstandardized evaluation techniques that use complex thought processes. Such alternatives are almost exclusively performance-based and criterion- referenced. Performance-based assessment is a form of testing that requires a student to create an answer or product or demonstrate a skill that displays his or her knowledge or abilities. Many types of performance assessments have been proposed and implemented, including projects or group projects, essays or writing samples, open-ended problems, interviews or oral presentations, science experiments, computer simulations, constructed-response questions, and portfolios.

Authentic Assessments

Authentic assessment is usually considered a specific kind of performance assessment, although the term is sometimes used interchangeably with performance-based or alternative assessment. The authenticity in the name derives from the focus of this evaluation technique to directly measure complex, real world, relevant tasks. Authentic assessments can include writing and revising papers, providing oral analyses of world events, collaborating with others on a debate team, and conducting research. Such tasks require the student to synthesize knowledge and create polished, thorough, and justifiable answers. The increased validity of authentic assessments stems from their relevance to classroom material and applicability to real-life scenarios.

Whether or not specifically performance-based or authentic, alternative assessments achieve greater reliability through the use of predetermined and specific evaluation criteria. Rubrics are often used for this purpose and can be created by one counselor or a group of counselors involved in similar assessments. (A rubric is a set of guidelines for scoring which generally states all of the dimensions being assessed, contains a scale, and helps the grader place the given work on the scale.) Creating a rubric is often time-consuming, but it can help clarify the key features of the performance or product and allows for more consistency. Following is an example of an assignment and a rubric for assessing students' written responses.

An elementary school counselor completed a unit on bullying with fifth-grade students. She instructed the students to write a one-page paper explaining

What is bullying? What should you do at school when a bully bothers you? How can students help stop bullying at school? Why do people bully others? Give examples to illustrate your points.

- A "4" paper addresses the questions asked of the student. The paper clearly shows an appropriate awareness of bullying. It is well-organized and contains details and insights to engage the reader.
- A "3" paper addresses the questions asked of the student; however, it contains vague or inarticulate language. It is missing some details and examples.
- A "2" paper does not fully address the questions asked of the student, which cause the paper to be rambling and disjointed. The paper demonstrates an incomplete or inadequate understanding of conflict resolution.
- A "1" paper barely addresses the questions. Awareness of the topic is missing. The general idea may be conveyed, but details, facts, examples, or descriptions are lacking.

Counselor in Action

Collect data regarding your school, students, policies, and so forth. Possible data sources might include school's college-going rate, students' test scores, attendance rates, suspension rates, percentage of students in special education (by race and gender), and percentage of students in gifted and talented program or courses (by race and gender). After retrieving and reviewing your data, respond to the following questions:

1. How is student performance described (by medians, quartiles, averages, aggregates, etc.)?
2. How are different groups of students performing? Which groups are meeting the targeted goals? What don't the data tell you? What other data do you need to get a better picture of what is going on?
3. What stakeholders might you need to talk to in order to better understand the data?
4. What are the implications for?
developing or revising school policies
revising school counselor practices and strategies

(Continued)

(Continued)

> reading literature
> visiting other schools
> revising, eliminating, adding programs
> dialogues with experts
> professional development
>
> ---
>
> SOURCE: Adapted from *Using Data to Close the Achievement Gap*, by Ruth S. Johnson. Copyright 2002.

QUESTIONS TO CONSIDER

1. What types of data do you collect now? Discuss how that data can be used to highlight inequities or to illustrate your program's effectiveness.

2. Who or what office in your district collects, analyzes, and disseminates data? Where are they located? How can you access their data? Visit the person or the office and retrieve more information about your district's data.

3. Review the data in Figure 6.2. What does the data tell you? What types of patterns and trends do you see? What types of programs might you initiate based on the data? What additional data would you want?

7 Challenging Bias

The cornerstone of a social justice–focused school counseling program is the ability of the school counselor to recognize and challenge bias and oppression in the school setting. When discussing school reform initiatives, it is apparent that most of these initiatives are based on the critical consciousness of the educator leading the initiative. In other words, the people involved must truly have passion for social justice and an ability to identify oppressive behavior when they see it. There is no way that a school counselor can work from a social justice framework without having the ability and willingness to challenge biased views, practices, and behaviors.

In this chapter I explore the difficult yet liberating process of challenging bias in schools. I offer guidelines to help school counselors challenge bias in their school settings and discuss human rights education and its applicability to the work of social justice–focused school counseling.

GUIDELINES FOR CHALLENGING BIAS

It's happened many times in schools: little comments about "those people" or jokes about students' nationality ("spic" jokes, "trailer trash" jokes) or cruel comments about an individual's physical characteristics. All of these types of incidents perpetuate stereotypes, bias, and contradict social justice. Bias reinforces oppressive attitudes and creates an environment of unjust policies and inequitable practices. Counselors who work from a social justice framework do not accept or tolerate bias. Ignoring bias will not make it go away, and silence can send the message that you are in agreement with such attitudes and behaviors. Social justice–focused counselors make it clear that they do not tolerate any actions that demean or devalue any person or group.

Be Aware of Your Own Attitudes, Stereotypes, and Expectations

We have all been socialized to believe many myths and generalizations. None of us remains untouched by the discriminatory messages in our society. However, only a few of us are honest about our biases and prejudiced thoughts. Social justice–focused school counselors do not avoid discussions about bias, prejudice, or any topic related to people's differences. To confront bias, social justice–focused school counselors are not defensive when their biased behavior is pointed out to them. For example, a student calls a counselor "racist." The counselor does not get angry; instead, the counselor validates the student's opinion and initiates an open discussion with the student about his concerns. The counselor does not discount the student's accusation. To determine and understand your assumptions about different groups, complete Exercise 7.1.

Actively Listen To and Learn From Others' Experiences

Counselors working from a social justice framework never trivialize or deny people's concerns and they make an effort to see situations through others' eyes. Parents from culturally diverse backgrounds will often perceive situations and activities at the school very differently from school personnel. Their varying views of what happens in a school are likely due to parents' diverse experiences with schools and school personnel. In many cases, students and their parents will use their experiences with discrimination and oppression to frame their understanding of what happens in schools. Counselors must be willing to listen and validate others' perceptions as well as learn from what others tell them. The following example illustrates this point.

Mr. Johnson, an African American father of a first-grade student, is very active in his daughter's schooling. He comes to the school regularly to talk to the staff and to pick up his daughter. Because the PTO is lacking diversity, the counselor asks Mr. Johnson to attend the next PTO meeting because they will be discussing a new reading initiative. Mr. Johnson attends the meeting and is very vocal in his skepticism of the reading initiative. He believes the initiative encourages ability grouping and tracking (see Chapter 8 for a definition of these terms). The other PTO members were excited about the initiative and were angry that Mr. Johnson had a different view. Moreover, they resented that he was invited to the meeting, considering him to not be a "part of their group." The PTO members

Exercise 7.1   Becoming Aware of Our Biases and Prejudices

I believe that . . .

1. African American students are _____

2. Asian students can _____

3. White students are _____

4. Native American students tend to _____

5. Latino students tend to _____

6. In school, girls tend to _____

7. In school, boys tend to _____

8. Disabled students _____

9. Gay and lesbian students are _____

10. If a school is predominately African American, it is _____

11. If a school is predominately White, it is _____

12. If I were offered a counseling position in an all-Latino high school, I would _____ because _____

13. If my children were zoned to attend a predominately African American school, I would _____

14. If my children were zoned to attend a predominately White school, I would _____

became noticeably angry with Mr. Johnson and interrupted his statements repeatedly. Mr. Johnson became extremely upset and stormed out of the meeting. "You all don't want to hear from me!" he stated as he left the meeting. The counselor voiced her concerns about the group's treatment of Mr. Johnson. She then called Mr. Johnson and validated his concerns about the reading initiative. She invited him to come speak to the administrator about his concerns.

The counselor, in the preceding vignette, understood that Mr. Johnson's perceptions of the reading initiative were likely based on his cultural and racial experiences. Because students-of-color have been historically oppressed by ability grouping and tracking, the reading initiative's grouping component was a "red flag" for Mr. Johnson. The school counselor should be applauded in this case because she realized the value of Mr. Johnson's ideas and views and she persisted in getting his voice heard by school personnel. Her actions also sent the message to the PTO that the school values all parents' concerns. The counselor and administrator later discovered that Mr. Johnson's views were closely aligned with other parents in the school community.

Acknowledge and Appreciate Diversity, Don't Just Tolerate It!

It is critical for counselors and other educators to acknowledge diversity and to point out the rich differences among staff and students. Acknowledging obvious differences is not the problem, but placing negative value judgments on those differences is! Social justice–focused counselors don't tolerate differences, they appreciate and celebrate differences.

Be Aware of Your Own Hesitancies to Intervene

Counselors will often hear, experience, or witness an oppressive act or statement in schools. What do you do? Do you hesitate? Feel nervous and then hesitate? A school counselor working from a social justice framework might hesitate to intervene but will surely challenge the act or statement. Here are four simple steps to follow when challenging a person or group regarding an oppressive statement or act:

1. *Take a breath*. It takes courage to challenge oppression because it will likely cause discomfort.

2. *Name the act*. Tell them exactly what they just did and name the oppression they contributed to (e.g., "What you just said is sexist").

3. *Give information as to why the act was offensive or oppressive.* For example, a counselor might state "Dave, your comment that girls should not be scientists is sexist because you are sending the message that it is not socially acceptable for girls to enter the science professions. You are not respecting girls' right to freely choose a career."

4. *Give direction and model good behavior.* Tell the person what they should do about it. For example, a counselor might say to Dave, "I've read a lot about gender bias in schools. I'll gladly share some information with you." Or a counselor may say to a colleague, "I've worked hard to learn to pronounce my students' names. I'll be happy to help you learn them, too."

The key to challenging others' biased comments and actions is to be as direct as possible. It is not a good idea to yell or to let one's anger take over. Yelling and screaming will only give the individual a chance to change the focus to your behavior rather than their oppressive behavior. You might want to ask the person for clarification, "Why do you say that?" "Are you saying that everyone should feel this way?" "Help me understand your attitude, I'm not understanding why you feel this way?" Remember, most people make changes when they are pushed out of their comfort zones and they are forced to evaluate why they are uncomfortable.

Thinking About . . . Challenging Bias

Respond to the following items:

1. Joan, a middle-school counselor, overhears a group of teachers making crude comments about a student's two mothers. One teacher states, "Those women should be banned from our school. I think it is horrible that they are allowed to participate on the PTO Board. Who wants to plan a pizza party with a bunch of dykes?" What should Joan do?

2. Alice and Judy are counselors at a high school with a science and math magnet program. The magnet program consists of primarily White and Asian students (96%), whereas the remainder of the student body is primarily African American and Latino (95%). Each spring, Alice and Judy make trips to promote the magnet program at middle schools with large numbers of White and Asian students. When you ask them why they do not visit some of the other middle schools in the district, they comment that "students at the other middle schools would never be successful in our magnet program." How would you challenge them?

Expect Tension and Conflict

Culturally insensitive and biased issues are unlikely to change without some struggle and resistance. Social justice–focused counselors understand that tension and conflict are positive forces that can foster change and growth. Therefore, social justice–focused counselors do not avoid confronting oppression because they fear conflict. They learn to manage the tension and conflict.

Work Collectively With Others

Social justice–focused counselors organize and support community efforts that combat prejudice and oppression. Social change is a long-term struggle and it's easy to get discouraged, but by working together, school counselors have strength and vision to make a difference. See the following for social justice Web sites and resources.

Social Justice Resources for Schools

To promote social justice in schools, counselors and teachers need resources for planning schoolwide programs, classroom lessons, and group activities. Below is a list of organizations and Web sites that distribute resources to schools:

www.tolerance.org	Southern Poverty Law Center
www.esrnational.org	Educators for Social Responsibility
crede.berkeley.edu/index.html	Center for Research on Education, Diversity, & Excellence
www.nccp.org	National Center for Children in Poverty
www.teachersagainstprejudice.org	Teachers Against Prejudice
www.ccsf.edu/Resources/Tolerance	Lessons in Tolerance

SOCIAL JUSTICE EDUCATION IN SCHOOLS

The main aim for a social justice–focused school counselor is to create an educational environment that encourages students to have public conversations about social justice. According to sociologist Pierre Bourdieu, every youngster brings rich "cultural capital" to the classroom: subtleties of language, artistic preferences, unique knowledge bases, and links to resources (Fowler, 1997). Nevertheless, classrooms and schools often do not value, acknowledge, or use the cultural capital of some groups of students. This makes some students feel as if they have no acceptable way to express themselves and share their cultural capital in the school setting.

Schools can either cultivate social justice and its composite issues—appreciating diversity, promoting equity, advancing broad-mindedness, and encouraging voice and expression—or they can suppress it. The following scenarios illustrate counselor responses that devalued students' perspectives and alternative responses that recognize and honor the students' points of view.

Scenario 1: Ignoring What Students Say

In a high-performing school district, Malik's counselor introduced the concept of *community* through classroom lessons. The counselor asked the students to identify an individual who provided a valuable service to the people in their community. Malik, a bright and articulate African American student, eagerly raised his hand and said that his father's car detailer, Eric, cleaned his father's car and some of his father's friends' cars. He stated that he does a good job and was very helpful and nice. The counselor, who had been listing jobs on the board under the label "Important Services" did not list the occupation on the board. She thanked Malik and then moved on to another student. Malik's counselor had preconceptions about important community services and car detailing was not among these services.

Did Malik leave the session with a diminished view of the role and value of car detailing? Maybe or maybe not. However, what certainly occurred was the devaluing of Malik's perspective. In contrast, the counselor could have asked Malik to explain how car detailing is an important community service. After his explanation, she could then add the job to the board. With this response, the counselor would have honored and validated Eric's work and Malik's perspective.

Scenario 2: Transposing What Students Say

A sixth-grade newcomers group was engaging in a lively discussion about their new neighborhoods. The counselor asked the students to describe what they liked best about their neighborhoods. Juan, a Chicano student who had moved to the suburban community from a low-income housing project, said that he liked his new room and backyard but he missed his old neighborhood, especially sharing a room with his cousin and playing on the block with his cousin and friends. The counselor thanked him for his contribution and then proceeded to explain to the group how fortunate Juan was to have a community that provided him with more space, safer living conditions, and good schools. By changing Juan's feelings about his former and current neighborhoods, his counselor essentially disregarded Juan's beliefs about the quality of community life in his urban housing project.

Juan's counselor could have honored and validated Juan's views by asking more questions about what life was like in his previous neighborhood and by asking Juan whether it would be possible to re-create some of those advantages in his present neighborhood. The counselor could have reflected on his relationship with his former friends and cousin. His sense of belonging was fulfilled in his former neighborhood!

Scenario 3: Marginalizing What Students Say

While conducting a classroom guidance lesson on great leaders of the twentieth century, Sharon, a tenth-grade African American, offered Malcolm X's name as a great leader, adding that her parents had several of his books in their home. The counselor reiterated that she wanted "great leaders" and that Malcolm X was not a great leader. She suggested that Sharon refer to some library books for other ideas.

The counselor's adherence to leaders in books eliminated a discussion and forestalled critical thinking on the topic. Sharon learned a lot through this interaction, but probably not about leadership. Did Sharon learn that her parents don't know what they think they know? Or that library books dictate what is valued not only in the school but also in the larger society? Maybe or maybe not, but we do know that Sharon's perspective was devalued.

Instead the counselor could have asked Sharon to explain the characteristics of Malcolm X that made him a great leader. The counselor's question directs attention to the definition of *greatness* and the value that society attributes to the cultural capital of certain leaders. Also, it reinforces that "greatness" is subjective and culturally defined.

QUESTIONS TO CONSIDER

1. Describe and discuss a time when you heard a biased or prejudiced statement or comment made by a colleague. What did you do? What do you wish you had done? How would the colleague have reacted?

2. Do you believe the achievement gap is primarily caused by biased beliefs about students of particular ethnic groups? Why or why not?

3. Which cultural group do you have the most difficulty working with? Why?

8 Coordinating Student Services and Support

As a country we need to realize the long-term results of tracking. Then we must commit ourselves to educate all students. Only a change in philosophy of education—away from the factory model—can bring about needed results. Our country will not survive in its present form with anything less.

—Launa Ellison
Clara Barton Open School
Minneapolis

Central to the success of high-achieving schools is a school culture that supports students and provides services to them that enhance their academic achievement. Student support services in schools include academic support for students with special needs, the promotion of rigorous courses that support future goals, and regular contact with organizations that can provide support for students' academic and emotional development. This chapter includes an overview of the types of student support that cultivate success for all students, particularly those students who are at risk.

COLLABORATING WITH COMMUNITY ORGANIZATIONS AND SOCIAL SERVICE AGENCIES

When students struggle with academics, contributing factors often emanate from community or familial problems. For this reason, school counselors that work from a social justice framework must provide students and their families with the support they need to improve their condition. Although counselors are trained to provide an array of services to their students and families, sometimes the services that counselors can provide during the school day are insufficient. So counselors must then turn to community resources to support their counseling programs. Most communities have an abundance of resources that are available to parents. The goal of collaborating with community agencies is to provide students and families with culturally appropriate resources that will further empower the student's academic development. The typical community agencies that counselors refer students and their families to include community health agencies, mental health agencies, and social services (i.e., child abuse agencies, family service agencies, and private practitioners). Social justice–focused school counselors keep a record of which agencies offer the best services (based on feedback from students and parents) and they seek out information regarding the agencies' ability to meet the needs of various cultural groups. For instance, a counselor may discover that a popular family counseling agency in the school community has no Spanish-speaking therapists. As such, the counselor does not refer her Spanish-speaking families to that agency until they hire bilingual staff.

In order to compile a list of agencies and private practitioners that can assist families, school counselors should visit local agency sites. While on these visits, counselors should note answers to the following questions:

- What is the name of the agency or practice?
- Where are they located? Get contact phone numbers.
- What is their mission or purpose, including who they serve?
- What is their fee structure?
- Who provides client services (interns, licensed professionals, paid staff, volunteers, etc.)?
- How does a client access services? Ask the person you talk with to walk you through each step a client goes through from the moment he or she picks up the phone and calls. Who answers the phone? What happens next?
- How does the agency accommodate clients who speak little or no English?

- How does the agency address its clients' cultural differences?
- Does the agency gather data to determine the effectiveness of their services? If so, what data do they have and what does it say about their efficacy?

IMPLEMENTING SCHEDULING PRACTICES THAT ENCOURAGE RIGOROUS COURSE TAKING

Scheduling is often perceived by school counselors as a task they would rather not do. However, scheduling students' classes is one of the most powerful tasks that a counselor can implement. If a secondary school counselor is concerned about social justice and equity, then scheduling becomes an important and critical function of his or her job. Secondary school master schedules can include not only periods and subjects offered, but also who teaches what course and the numbers of students in each course. According to Johnson (2002), the master schedule can be analyzed for the following details:

- The types and numbers of courses being offered. Are courses being offered that will prepare students to be competitive and provide eligibility for college? Are higher-level courses increasing over time and remedial courses decreasing? What is the ratio of vocational to academic courses?

- Other inquiries include monitoring the number of students in each section of a course at different points in time. For instance, what is the enrollment in geometry in September, November, February, and June? Are the numbers stable or dwindling? What do the numbers look like at the higher levels? Which teachers are teaching at different levels from year to year?

- Master schedules can be compared from year to year and within years to give a picture of the direction the school is moving in. This is important in schools that are increasing academic rigor and addressing equity issues. It is important to note that year-round schools with large numbers of English as a second language students often place them all on one track. This scheduling frequently denies these students opportunities to take higher-level courses.

Counselors should also examine the master schedule for trends that limit students' access to opportunities. For instance, the distribution of courses should be examined to ensure that higher-level courses are offered so that all students have an opportunity to take them. Other practices that should be examined include

- distribution of teacher quality,
- distribution of resources,
- distribution of electives
- distribution of extracurricular activities,
- distribution of knowledge about opportunities for college or higher education.

It is through scheduling that a social justice–focused counselor can advocate for more rigorous course taking among low-achieving and low-motivated students. Counselors working from a social justice perspective allot time to meet with each of their advisees regarding their schedules. These student conferences provide time for counselors and students to discuss future goals, student strengths, and student goals. Below is an outline of what might be discussed at a scheduling conference:

1. Discussion of current grades and courses.

2. Discussion of college and career goals.

3. Discussion of students' strengths and areas of concern.

4. Discussion of future schedule: What courses will help the student attain his or her goals? What courses might be challenging? Why? Discuss supports that the student needs.

5. Devise plan of action for future (e.g., schedule for next 2 semesters, time line for taking important tests such as PSAT, SAT, schedule for academic support).

Counselors should have brochures, pamphlets, and other information packets ready for students at the conferences. It's also a good idea for counselors to schedule the conferences in at least 30-minute intervals so that there is time for discussion and relationship building with the student. Counselors must be cognizant of some students' need for more time and plan accordingly. As an example, Jordan, an eleventh-grade honors student will be a first-generation college student if he attends college in two years. Because his family lacks information about the college application process, the counselor allots extra time for his scheduling conference so that they can discuss his schedule and college application deadlines. The same counselor scheduled more time for a student failing all of her ninth-grade courses.

For those students who are from families that lack college information, student conferences are a great time to provide information or at least to inform students of where they can retrieve information. Although counselors have large student caseloads, the process of scheduling should not be taken lightly because it is during this process that a counselor can make a difference between a student being college or career prepared and a student dropping out or not having the appropriate coursework for college or a career.

Thinking About . . . the Master Schedule

If you are a secondary counselor, examine your school's master schedule. Do you see any trends related to when courses are offered? Which teachers teach higher-level courses? Lower-level courses?

Say No to Gatekeeping

School counselors are often referred to as "gatekeepers." *Gatekeeping* is a process of course selection and enrollment, beginning in middle school and extending through high school, that limits student access to a challenging curriculum. African American and Latino students are more likely to report reluctance to use counselors because they perceive them as gatekeepers (Gandara & Bial, 2001). In addition, school counselors have been reported to place students-of-color and poor students in noncollege track classes, effectively shutting these groups of students out of postsecondary educational opportunities. In essence, gatekeeping limits the opportunities for students to enroll in the courses necessary for college admission.

Say No to Tracking

Counseling is often tied to the track placement of students. The process of placing students in courses that will ultimately lead them to postsecondary educational opportunities (e.g., college) or to noncollege placement courses is called *tracking*. Tracking involves categorizing students into distinct groups according to particular measures of intelligence or performance for purposes of teaching and learning. Once sorted and classified, students are provided with curriculum and instruction deemed suited to their ability and matched to spoken or unspoken assessments of each student's future. If students are not in the college track, they will not receive college information or college advising. Research has dramatically demonstrated that this practice has created as many problems as it was designed to solve. Tracking does not result in the equal and equitable distribution of effective schooling for all students. Instead, tracking allocates the most valuable school experiences—including challenging and meaningful curriculum, engaging instruction, and high teacher expectations—to students who already have the greatest academic, economic, and social advantages, whereas students who face the greatest struggles in school and in life receive a more impoverished curriculum based on lower expectations for their capacity to learn.

Over time, students assigned to the lower levels move so much more slowly than those at the higher levels that differences that may have been real but not profound in the earlier grades become gigantic gaps in achievement, attitude, and self-esteem. Furthermore, the sorting of students into groups of "haves" and "have-nots" contradicts the concept of social justice and American values of schools as democratic communities that offer equal educational opportunity to all.

Untracking or de-tracking requires abandoning a strategy that sorts students according to individual weakness in favor of one that groups students for collective strength. It requires changing policies and methods for placing students in classes and programs. Methods for making decisions about student groupings or tracking typically include teacher recommendations, parent recommendations, student recommendations, test scores, and grades. These methods must be examined closely for inequities and biased practices. De-tracking also requires a shift from nurturing the ability of some children to cultivating effort, persistence, and pride in work in all children. It requires moving from a mindset that defines good education as a scarce resource, with the "best" reserved for the most "deserving," to one that envisions a society in which good education is abundant enough for all. Social justice–focused school counselors are committed to de-tracking and provoking a reconsideration of the purposes of education. In an era when knowledge is truly power, a redistribution of knowledge is both fair and necessary.

COORDINATING COLLEGE PREPARATION INTERVENTIONS

Because low-income students and students-of-color are often deprived of quality college preparation conditions in their K–12 schools, social justice-focused school counselors actively support students and their families through the college admissions process. Because disseminating information about colleges is not enough for students who are marginalized or from culturally and economically diverse backgrounds, social justice–focused school counselors in middle and high schools engage students and their families in college-going activities (e.g., rigorous courses, high academic standards). More specifically, social justice–focused school counselors do the following to prepare students for college admission:

- provide college preparation and admission activities that foster and support all students' college aspirations,
- help all parents understand their role in the college preparation process,
- support and influence students' decision making about college,
- help students realize the wide range of college options,
- present examples of successful applications, and
- maintain professional networks with college admission officers.

School counselors can include college-going activities in many formats— in small groups, individually, in classrooms, or in large group. The format can vary. The key is that students are getting early information and guidance about postsecondary options. Suggested college-going activities include the following:

- Arrange panel presentations by former students, community leaders, media personalities, professional athletes, college alumni, or other role models explaining the advantages of a college education.
- Have students visit a local college or university for a campus tour.
- Have students "shadow" a college student for a day.
- Have students complete a mock college application.
- Have students research and prepare reports on individual colleges.
- Have a college fair.
- Use college students to tutor or mentor middle- and high-school students.
- Offer elementary students tutoring on college campuses.
- Provide a workshop for parents on financial planning, strategies to pay for college, and the availability of financial aid (workshop for elementary, middle, and high-school parents).

COORDINATING TUTORING SERVICES

One of the most important student support services that social justice–focused counselors can ensure for students is tutoring services. One-on-one, adult-to-child tutoring is one of the most effective instructional strategies known (Slavin, 2002). However, providing tutoring services can be a costly proposition. Many schools have developed tutoring programs in which adult volunteers implement the tutoring. From a social justice perspective, counselors should be at the forefront of coordinating tutoring services for those students who are lagging in academic development and need extra support to maintain or catch up in their grades. Social justice-focused counselors can play an active role in determining the diversity of the tutors. Counselors should try to ensure that the tutors' demographics are similar to the tutees.

PARTICIPATING ON INDIVIDUALIZED EDUCATION PROGRAM COMMITTEES

One of the most powerful and significant student support committees in a school is the individualized education program (IEP) committee, the committee that makes recommendations for student placement in special education. The issue of disproportionate placement of students-of-color in special education continues to be documented at the national level and in many state and local education agencies. Disproportionate placement generally refers to the representation of a particular group of students at a rate different than that found in the general population. Student placements can be considered disproportionate if they are overrepresented or underrepresented when comparing their presence in a particular class or category with their representation in the general population.

By far the greatest attention in the literature has been given to the overrepresentation of students-of-color in special education. A recent report on special education by the Civil Rights Project at Harvard University (Losen & Orfield, 2002) found that African American youngsters are more often classified as needing special education, and once they are classified they are not likely to be placed in mainstream classrooms or returned to regular education. In addition, African American and Native American students are more than 2.9 times more likely to be labeled "mentally retarded" and 1.9 times more likely to be identified as having an emotional problem (U.S. Department of Education, 2004). The U.S. Department of Education report indicated that racial bias is clearly playing a major role in the overrepresentation of African American students in special education.

Because of the disproportionate number of students-of-color in special education, counselors should play the role of advocate not only on IEP committees but in the entire school and community. Social justice–focused counselors advocate locally and nationally for the best services for disabled students and they advocate for fair, unbiased decision making regarding special education placements. Because the realities of disproportionality in special education suggest that race matters, counselors working for social justice advocate for policies that state what is an unacceptable number of students-of-color in special education.

Social justice–focused school counselors also advocate for parents to have a voice at IEP meetings. In many cases, parents and families are confused by the terminology used at IEP meetings, and they are unfamiliar with their rights and options. School counselors can act as parent advocates and ask questions that they feel the parent might want to know.

PARTICIPATING ON GIFTED AND TALENTED COMMITTEES

As is the case with special education committees, social justice–focused counselors also act as advocates on gifted and talented identification committees. For many years, educational professionals have been concerned about the underrepresentation of children from cultural, linguistic, and low-income backgrounds in traditional gifted programs. These children, many of whom show potential for superior performance in areas that are not easily assessed by traditional ability measures, have not been provided with opportunities that elicit their gifts and talents and encourage them to maximize that potential. The National Educational Longitudinal Study (NELS) of 1988 looked at eighth graders throughout the nation and found that 65% of the public schools (serving 75% of all public school eighth graders), had some kind of opportunity for gifted and talented students. The NELS study found that about 8.8% of all eighth-grade public school students participated in gifted and talented programs, and that some minority groups were more likely to be served than others. Economically disadvantaged students were significantly underserved, according to NELS data. On the basis of this data, it is imperative that social justice–focused school counselors advocate for identification policies and criteria that make it more likely that a diverse group of students will be represented in gifted programs.

The best identification practices rely on multiple criteria to look for students with gifts and talents. Multiple criteria involve

- multiple types of information, including, for example, indicators of student's cognitive abilities, academic achievement, performance in a variety of settings, interests, creativity, motivation; and learning characteristics and behaviors;

- multiple sources of information (e.g., test scores, school grades, and comments by classroom teachers, specialty area teachers, counselors, parents, peers, and the students themselves); and

- multiple time periods to ensure that students are not missed by "one shot" identification procedures that often take place at the end of second or third grade.

We must also ensure that standardized measures use normative samples appropriate to the students being tested, taking into account factors such as ethnicity, language, or the presence of a disability.

The use of multiple criteria does not mean the creation of multiple hurdles to jump in order to be identified as gifted. Social justice-focused school counselors look for students with outstanding potential in a variety of ways and at a variety of time periods to ensure that no child who needs services provided through gifted education is missed. Data collected through the use of multiple criteria give us indicators of a student's need for services.

QUESTIONS TO CONSIDER

1. School counselors have been accused of keeping specific groups of students from gifted programming and college-preparatory courses. Do you believe this is true? Why does this happen? Is it based on biased beliefs about cultural groups?

2. What student services and support do counselors at your school offer? Have those services been helpful to students? How do you know?

3. What are your thoughts regarding the role of counselors in scheduling? Should counselors continue to do scheduling? Or should scheduling be a task for another school professional (e.g., aide, dean of students)?

9 Doing the Right Thing

*Developing a Social
Justice–Focused School
Counseling Program*

True peace is not the absence of tension but the presence of justice.

—Dr. Martin Luther King, Jr.

When Travis Middle School's principal asked Karen, the new school counseling chairperson, what her vision for the school counseling program would be, she was not sure how to respond. Karen realized that she hadn't thought about a vision or a plan for her program. She hadn't discussed a vision with the existing school counselors and they hadn't talked about what they would like to see take place in the next 3 years, 5 years, or 10 years at Travis. They were merely going to continue what had always been done.

In the past, Karen developed yearly goals for her guidance supervisor but she wrote these goals mostly for the benefit of central administration's expectations. There was no real passion or guiding principles behind her goals. Sure, Karen wanted to help students, she wanted them to succeed, but she had no guiding principles or philosophy for ensuring student success. Most of Karen's colleagues (i.e., teachers, specialists) had no idea what was in the school counseling plan, what counselors expected of students, or what their philosophy of counseling entailed. Her plans very rarely included clearly stated goals for student achievement, a vision for what she wanted for the total school, plans for changing school culture, or plans for challenging barriers to students' success. Yet, Karen followed the American School Counselor Association model and her district's stated guidance curriculum. Karen worked hard but there was nothing to show for it, no evidence, no statement of what she truly believed in and what she was passionate about. Karen's case is not rare. There are many school counselors who are well-intentioned and do wonderful work, but they work without fire, passion, or simply put, without a philosophy for what they believe schools and school counselors can do to ensure social justice for *all* kids.

This book has offered a place for school counselors to begin their quest for a vision. The social justice approach to school counseling is more about a paradigm shift in the way school counselors think about what they do. It's a shift from "I provide services that I *think* my students need" to "I provide services that are based on what I *know* students and their families need." It's a shift from "I treat *all of* my students the same regardless of their cultural background" to "I work with students based on their unique cultural backgrounds and needs." A shift from thinking that cultural differences are a *problem to* thinking that cultural differences are an *asset*. A shift from assuming that the achievement gap is just "the way things are" to "the achievement gap is a result of unjust policies, practices, and perceptions." The social justice approach, in essence, is a commitment to making things fair and right for all students!

Although developing a social justice–focused school counseling program sounds like the logical "good" thing to do, there is a price. Changing existing policies to policies that bring about equity, opening our school doors to the marginalized and oppressed, and challenging bias are all behaviors that will create tension and uneasiness among our colleagues. Change is difficult for everyone, but changing the landscape of schools that have historically worked in favor of the dominant racial and income group will surely cause resistance. A counselor and good friend of mine once told me, "Why should I change this AP policy for more inclusion when it will only work against *my* child getting a spot in a class or a seat at a competitive university?" She was being very honest with me and reflected the reason why social justice is so slow to occur in schools. However, if we want to do the right thing, we put aside our selfish and personal gains and focus on the good for all. I believe that if we focus on the good for all, we will all reap the benefits. Remember, if we have better education for all, we will have more job opportunities for all, less poverty, less anger, and less frustration, which means less crime and violence in communities.

In this chapter, I will offer a way for you to begin reflecting on your vision for a more social justice–focused school counseling program. First, however, you will need to assess your personal beliefs and skills with the several strategies and methods discussed in this book.

ASSESSING YOUR BELIEFS

To work from a social justice framework, you must tap into your beliefs about schools, school reform, student achievement, and social justice. Therefore, these questions should be discussed at length and reflected on before moving forward.

Counselor Belief Assessment

Discuss each of the following questions either individually or in small groups. Be honest and reflect on your responses. Record (i.e., audiotape) your responses and then go back and listen. You might be surprised at what you hear.

- In your opinion, what is the difference between equity and equality? How will you address equity and equality in your school counseling program?

- Describe how social justice is the driving force or guiding principle for your program. Are all children positively influenced by your program? Who doesn't benefit from your services? Why not?

- Reflect on equity and social justice. How do you define each?

- Do you believe that all students can achieve? What does *student success* mean to you?

- Why do you believe there is an achievement gap? What is your responsibility in closing the achievement gap?

- Why do some students achieve and others do not? Who do you believe can be high achievers?

- What are your cultural biases and prejudiced beliefs? How do these beliefs influence your decisions and practices?

- Do you agree or disagree with the following statements? "I believe that school counselors should be more social justice focused" and "I believe school counselors are partly responsible for the disparity in opportunities and access experienced by low-income and minority students."

ASSESSING YOUR SKILLS

The more skills and strategies you have mastered, the greater will be your possibility for success as a social justice–focused school counselor. The form beginning on the following page lists the skills and strategies related to the topics in this book. Three levels of mastery are presented and defined here: Rate yourself on each skill or strategy for your mastery level.

Identification Mastery: You are able to identify the skill or strategy through observation. You are aware of cultural differences that might relate to the skill.

Basic Mastery: You are able to engage in the skill or strategy. You can use the skill or strategy with students from different cultural groups.

Teaching Mastery: You can teach others to implement this skill or strategy.

ASSESSING YOUR STUDENTS' NEEDS

After assessing your skills, next assess the needs of your students by analyzing existing data at your school. In a big binder, keep ongoing records of school data and your notes regarding critical areas of concern. Your records should include charts that resemble the charts in Tables 9.1–9.3.

When reviewing the data, search for trends and patterns over at least a 3-year period. For instance, in Table 9.1, over a 5-year period it is clear that Native American, Latino, and African American students' grade point averages are significantly less than those of White students. As a school counselor, you would ask, "Why is this trend occurring?" "What other data would help me understand the problem better?"

Examine the data in Table 9.2. What are the trends in the identification of gifted and talented students? Do all children have access to this special program? What is happening during the identification process? What is the policy for identifying gifted and talented students? Is there bias in the policy?

And in Table 9.3, the wide disparity among grades distributed by math teachers is obvious. A school counselor should ask then, "Are all students getting a fair opportunity in basic math?" This indicates a need for more data work and dialogue among teachers and administrators about what is the acceptable percentage of failing grades from one course.

Skills Assessment Form

Skill or strategy	Level of mastery (I, B, T)	What will you do to acquire this skill?
1. Ability to identify when there are cultural differences		
2. Ability to determine cultural appropriateness of counseling approach		
3. Ability to discern whether a student's behavior is cultural rather than pathological		
4. Ability to speak the language of students		
5. Ability to locate translators or bilingual counselors		
6. Ability to assess students' abilities and career development in a culturally appropriate manner		
7. Ability to determine when culture negatively influences a counseling relationship		
8. Ability to build trusting relationships with culturally diverse students		
9. Ability to Instill critical consciousness in students		
10. Ability to implement empowerment counseling		
11. Ability to interview students and their families in a culturally sensitive manner		
12. Ability to assess a school's culture		
13. Ability to advocate for students during consultation		
14. Ability to challenge teachers' and parents' culturally inappropriate attitudes and behaviors		
15. Ability to develop partnerships with community organizations		

(Continued)

(Continued)

Skill or strategy	Level of mastery (I, B, T)	What will you do to acquire this skill?
16. Ability to work with parents using a relational narrative or style		
17. Ability to recognize when others' communication style is negatively influencing relationships with parents of culturally diverse backgrounds		
18. Ability to ask critical questions regarding school policies, demographics, student achievement, and so forth		
19. Ability to determine types of data needed for critical questions		
20. Ability to disaggregate and analyze data		
21. Ability to present data to colleagues		
22. Ability to use data to advocate for school change		
23. Ability to evaluate school counseling interventions		
24. Ability to challenge bias of others		
25. Ability to integrate social justice–focused education in counseling curriculum		
26. Ability to implement scheduling practices that encourage students' academic potential		
27. Ability to coordinate tutoring and other student support services		
28. Ability to advocate for students.		
29. Ability to de-track students from non-college-going tracks		

Table 9.1 High-School Grade Point Averages by Race

Race/ethnicity	2002	2003	2004	2005	2006
Native American	1.96	2.27	2.30	2.31	2.30
Latino	2.0	2.31	2.41	2.42	2.43
White	3.20	2.99	3.43	3.45	3.43
African American	2.12	2.32	2.33	2.33	2.35

Table 9.2 Third-Grade Enrollment in Gifted and Talented Program by Race

Race/ethnicity	2004	2005	2006
African American	0	1	0
White	10	9	9
Latino	3	2	2
Asian	5	6	5
Native American	0	2	1

Table 9.3 Grade Analysis by Teacher for Basic Sixth-Grade Math

Teacher	Total # of students	A's	B's	C's	D's	F's
A	30	4 (13%)	6 (20%)	10 (33%)	4 (13%)	6 (20%)
B	35	0	0	4 (11%)	4 (11%)	27 (77%)
C	33	5 (15%)	7 (21%)	5 (15%)	12 (36%)	4 (12%)
D	30	1 (3%)	3 (10%)	2 (7%)	8 (27%)	16 (53%)

MY VISION FOR MY SCHOOL COUNSELING PROGRAM

After reviewing your data and considering your notes on students' needs, it is time to think about how equity and social justice will influence your school counseling program. The worksheet, "My Vision for a Social Justice–Focused School Counseling Program," was developed to help you envision aspects of your social justice–focused school counseling program and its outcomes. It should help you organize your program around the six key functions outlined in this book.

Share your worksheet responses with administrators, fellow counselors, parents, teachers, and other stakeholders who are interested in your program and school reform. They will love your new program's focus!

CONCLUDING REMARKS

The most critical problem facing U.S. schools is the persistence of a pernicious achievement gap. Fortunately, there is convincing evidence that the achievement gap can be closed if certain components are present—leadership, accountability, data-driven programs, and parent involvement. Because of their unique position in schools, school counselors can play a critical role in closing the achievement gap by addressing the six key functions outlined in this book—counseling and intervention planning; consultation; connecting schools, families, and communities; collecting and using data; challenging bias; and coordinating student services and support (six C's). Implementing school counseling with an emphasis on these functions is not simple, but it is attainable.

The process of discovering and challenging inequities in schools is difficult and time-consuming. Once you are aware of injustice and inequities, it can be burdensome and tiring. Remember, however, that your attention to social justice can change the lives of many students and their families and can make the difference in our country's failing educational system. The key is that we change how we think about and do our jobs as school counselors. Good luck in your journey.

My Vision for a Social Justice–Focused School Counseling Program

1. My main goals for students, as a result of interacting and working with school counselors are _____

2. At this time, there are student inequities in my school (e.g., disproportionate number of students-of-color in special education, lack of girls in advanced math classes, lack of English language learners represented in the gifted program). List below. Include data to support these statements. _____

3. My vision for students is _____

4. Student achievement will be evident as a result of these school counseling activities: _____ (Describe at least 5 activities or interventions)

5. To promote social justice, I will work with teachers to _____ (e.g., communicate more effectively with parents-of-color, identify strengths in students)

6. To promote social justice, I will work with students to _____ (e.g., enhance their ethnic identity development, identify their strengths, identify their goals)

7. To promote social justice, I will work with administrators to _____ (e.g., understand systemic oppression, understand data, promote the effectiveness of counseling interventions)

8. To promote social justice, I will work with parents _____ (e.g., to enhance their feelings of empowerment, to enhance their understanding of postsecondary options)

9. To promote social justice, I will work with communities to _____ (e.g., provide safety for children, provide resources for parents)

10. To promote social justice, I will collect and analyze these types of data

_____

(e.g., college enrollment, access to special programs, grades, attendance)

11. To promote social justice, I will change the school's culture to _____

12. To promote social justice, I will challenge bias in these areas _____ (e.g., special education identification, postsecondary options, teachers' low expectations)

13. As a result of these interventions (e.g., individual work, group work, classroom guidance, schoolwide initiatives, community initiatives, parent initiatives) students will be able to (list student outcomes; use SOARING format) _____

14. I want my school to become a place where _____ _____

RESOURCES

Resource A

Assessing School Equity

In a small group (e.g., school-based leadership team, group of counselors), answer each of the following questions to assess whether or not your school is addressing equity.

- Who is participating in classes? Are teachers paying attention to, asking probing questions of, and encouraging all students?
- Who gets access to technology and why?
- Are students being discouraged from speaking and writing in their native language and encouraged to give up their culture?
- Does the curriculum represent the contributions of all people (women and people-of-color, for example)?
- Are there accurate historical accounts of shameful periods of U.S. history (e.g., slavery, the treatment of Native Americans, the internment of Japanese Americans, anti-Semitism, and the eugenics movement)?
- Are there faculty role models for students? How does it affect students-of-color if most of the teachers they see are White?
- Do students talk with other student respectfully about important issues?
- Can students talk with each other about their problems? with teachers?
- How much harassment and teasing (of female students, of students-of-color, of gay students for example) goes on in the school?
- Are there friendships in the school across racial and class lines?
- Are students-of-color in positions of leadership?
- How do people explain the disproportionate failure or success by students-of-color, language-minority students, and students from low economic classes?
- When equity issues are raised, do teachers say, "We've already dealt with that" or "I don't see color"?

- Is it safe in the district to talk about sensitive issues such as racism, sexism, or homophobia? Are adults working to overcome their own biases?
- Do counselors understand how oppression works in our society?
- Do educators from different racial backgrounds communicate with each other? Are there friendships among educators across racial lines?
- Are teachers-of-color respected? Are they in positions of leadership?
- Do bilingual teachers have as much power in the school as regular teachers?
- How do teachers feel about their jobs? How does teacher morale affect students' school experiences?
- How does the pressure at the state and district level to improve test scores affect the way educators relate to students?
- Is the atmosphere of the school one of respect for students? How do teachers talk about students in the faculty room? What are their expectations? What kind of relationships do they have with students?
- Are parents of students-of-color and English-language learners present in school events and school board meetings? Are they represented on committees and on the school board? Do they feel they have a voice in the school and are respected members of the school community?
- Are translators always present at school meetings?
- Do teachers have professional development about relating to parents of different cultural backgrounds? Do teachers make an effort to support all parents' participation in their children's education (especially recent immigrants, parents-of-color, and parents from low socioeconomic classes)?
- Which parents have the most influence in the school?
- Does the scheduling of parent-teacher conferences discriminate against parents who have to work during the day?
- Are schools connected to the community in which they reside?
- How does the assessment system being used affect the achievement of students from underrepresented groups?
- How does the emphasis on raising test scores affect students from underrepresented groups?
- Are high stakes (including gifted-talented and placement) tests available in languages other than English?
- How do counseling practices affect student self-perception, performance? How are tracking policies affecting students' success?
- Does professional development at the school provide opportunities for educators to talk about the biases they encountered growing up and how that affects them? About how race, class, and gender bias affects teaching and learning? Are these issues treated in depth?

- Are teachers feeling empowered in planning and conducting their professional development?
- Are English-language learners receiving adequate support for learning academic subjects or is the emphasis on increasing reading scores impeding their learning of other subjects?
- Are high-level math and science classes taught bilingually or with sheltered methods?
- Do the most experienced and better-qualified teachers teach the classes with a disproportionately high number of White or affluent students?
- What is the ethnic distribution of teachers within the district?
- How are resources allocated to different schools within the district? Do schools with the most needy students also have the least-experienced teachers and worst equipment?
- Does the district and school leadership emphasize equity and practice what they preach? Are administrators providing both intellectual and emotional support to teachers for changing unequal success rates? Do teachers-of-color report having difficulty with one or more administrators?
- Do administrators and school boards support teachers' attempts to implement new curriculum or pedagogical approaches that provide access to the curriculum for more students? Do they provide encouragement for risk taking?

SOURCE: Reprinted from the 'Discussion Areas for Equity' of the National Coalition for Equity in Education, Department of Education, University of California, Santa Barbara, University of California, Santa Barbara, Ca 93106-7090. http://ncee.education.ucsb.edu/discussionareas.htm, with the permission of the Director Julian Weisglass.

Resource B

School Counselor Multicultural Competence Checklist

Developed by Cheryl Holcomb-McCoy, PhD

Multicultural Counseling

1. I can recognize when my beliefs and values are interfering with providing the best services to my students.

2. I can identify the cultural basis of my communication style.

3. I can discuss how culture affects the help-seeking behaviors of students.

4. I know when a counseling approach is culturally appropriate for a specific student.

5. I know when a counseling approach is culturally inappropriate for a specific student.

6. I can identify culturally appropriate interventions and counseling approaches (e.g., indigenous practices) with students.

7. I can list *at least* three barriers that prevent ethnic minority students from using counseling services.

8. I know when my helping style is inappropriate for a culturally different student.

9. I know when my helping style is appropriate for a culturally different student.

10. I can give examples of how stereotypical beliefs about culturally different persons impact the counseling relationship.

11. I know when my biases influence my service to students.

12. I know when specific cultural beliefs influence students' response to counseling.

13. I know when my helping style is inappropriate for a culturally different student.

Multicultural Consultation

14. I know when my culture is influencing the process of consultation.

15. I know when the consultee's (e.g., parent, teacher) culture is influencing the process of consultation.

16. I know when the race or culture of a student is a problem for a teacher.

17. I can initiate discussions related to race, ethnicity, and culture when consulting with teachers.

18. I can initiate discussions related to race, ethnicity, and culture when consulting with parents.

Understanding Racism and Student Resistance

19. I can define and discuss White privilege.

20. I can discuss how I (if European American or White) am privileged based on my race.

21. I can identify racist aspects of educational institutions.

22. I can define and discuss prejudice.

23. I can identify discrimination and discriminatory practices in schools.

24. I am able to challenge my colleagues when they discriminate against students.

25. I can define and discuss racism.

26. I can discuss the influence of racism on the counseling process.

27. I can discuss the influence of racism on the educational system in the United States.

28. I can help students determine whether a problem stems from racism or biases in others.

29. I understand the relationship between student resistance and racism.

30. I am able to discuss the relationship between student resistance and racism.

31. I include topics related to race and racism in my classroom guidance units.

32. I am able to challenge others' racist beliefs and behaviors.

33. I am able to identify racist and unjust policies in schools.

Understanding Racial and Ethnic Identity Development

34. I am able to discuss at least two theories of racial or ethnic identity development.

35. I can use racial and ethnic identity development theories to understand my students' problems and concerns.

36. I can assess my own racial and ethnic identity development in order to enhance my counseling.

37. I can help students explore their own racial identity development.

38. I can develop activities that enhance students' racial or ethnic identity.

39. I am able to discuss how racial identity may affect the relationships between students and educators.

Multicultural Assessment

40. I can discuss the potential bias of two assessment instruments frequently used in the schools.

41. I can evaluate instruments that may be biased against certain groups of students.

42. I am able to use test information appropriately with culturally diverse parents.

43. I can advocate for fair testing and the appropriate use of testing of children from diverse backgrounds.

44. I can identify whether or not the assessment process is culturally sensitive.

45. I can discuss how the identification stage of the assessment process might be biased against minority populations.

46. I can use culturally appropriate instruments when I assess students.

47. I am able to discuss how assessment can lead to inequitable opportunities for students.

Multicultural Family Interventions

48. I can discuss family counseling from a cultural-ethnic perspective.

49. I can discuss at least two ethnic group's traditional gender role expectations and rituals.

50. I anticipate when my helping style is inappropriate for a culturally different parent or guardian.

51. I can discuss culturally diverse methods of parenting and discipline.

52. I can discuss how class and economic level affect family functioning and development.

53. I can discuss how race and ethnicity influence family behavior.

54. I can identify when a school policy is biased against culturally diverse families.

Social Advocacy

55. I know of societal issues that affect the development of ethnic minority students.

56. When counseling, I am able to address societal issues that affect the development of ethnic minority students.

57. I can work with families and community members to reintegrate them with the school.

58. I can define *social change agent*.

59. I am able to be a social change agent.

60. I can discuss what it means to take an activist counseling approach.

61. I can intervene with students at the individual and systemic levels.

62. I can discuss how factors such as poverty and powerlessness have influenced the current conditions of at least two ethnic groups.

63. I am able to advocate for students who are being subjected to unfair practices.

64. I know how to use data as an advocacy tool.

Developing School-Family-Community Partnerships

65. I can discuss how school-family-community partnerships are linked to student achievement.

66. I am able to develop partnerships with families that are culturally different from me.

67. I am able to develop partnerships with agencies within my school's community.

68. I can define a school-family-community partnership.

69. I can discuss more than three types of parent involvement.

70. I am able to encourage the participation of ethnic minority parents in school activities.

71. I am able to work with community leaders and other resources in the community to assist with student and family concerns.

Understanding Cross-Cultural Interpersonal Interactions

72. I am able to discuss interaction patterns that might influence ethnic minority students' perceptions of inclusion in the school community.

73. I can solicit feedback from students regarding my interactions with them.

74. I can verbally communicate my acceptance of culturally different students.

75. I can nonverbally communicate my acceptance of culturally different students.

76. I am able to assess the manner in which I speak and the emotional tone of my interactions with culturally diverse students.

77. I am able to greet students and parents in a culturally acceptable manner.

78. I know of culturally insensitive topics or gestures.

Multicultural Career Assessment

79. I can develop and implement culturally sensitive career development activities in which materials are representative of all groups in a wide range of careers.

80. I can arrange opportunities for students to have interactions with ethnic minority professionals.

81. I am able to assess the strengths of multiple aspects of students' self-concept.

82. I can discuss differences in the decision-making styles of students.

83. I integrate my knowledge of varying decision-making styles when implementing career counseling.

84. I can integrate family and religious issues in the career counseling process.

85. I can use career assessment instruments that are sensitive to cultural differences of students.

86. I can discuss how work and career are viewed similarly and differently across cultures.

87. I can discuss how many career assessment instruments are inappropriate for culturally diverse students.

Multicultural Sensitivity

88. I am able to develop a close, personal relationship with someone of another race.

89. I am able to live comfortably with culturally diverse people.

90. I am able to be comfortable with people who speak another language.

91. I can make friends with people from other ethnic groups.

Resource C

School Culture Assessment

B elow are dimensions of a school's culture. To make an assessment of a school's culture, collect items and participate in the following activities in a school. Take notes and then summarize what you found.

1. *Artifacts:* Collect school memorabilia, yearbooks, faculty and student handbooks, master schedules, newsletters, memos, school newspaper, bulletin board items, and so forth. What themes do you see? What is valued in the school? Academics? Athletics?

2. *Rituals:* What types of events and activities occur at the school on a regular basis? Open houses, PTA or PTO meetings, celebrations, morning and afternoon announcements, programs, weekend events, seasonal events (holiday parties, programs), faculty meetings, and so forth. Attend at least four of these events. If there are very few rituals, what effect does that have on the school?

3. *Communication:* Interview faculty, parents, and students about how groups interact and communicate with one another. How are parents greeted when they enter the office? How does the school accommodate non-English-speaking students and parents?

4. *Collaboration:* Interview teachers, administrators, and parents regarding how they work with one another. Is there collaboration among teachers across grades and subjects?

5. *Innovation:* How are new concepts and strategies introduced and received? What new programs or curricula are being implemented in the school?

6. *Decision making:* How are decisions made? Describe the process of decision making? Is it shared?

7. *Leadership:* Who are the leaders in the school? Who has the "strongest voice"? Who has the weakest? Describe the administrators' leadership style.

Resource D

*Assessing Beliefs About
School-Family-Community
Partnership Involvement*

How involved do you believe school counselors should be in each of the following activities? (A Lot, Some, Not Too Much, None)

1. Working with a team of school staff, family, community members, or professionals (e.g., school mental health team)

2. Locating services and resources for students and their families in the community (e.g., mental health, nutrition, social services, and clothing)

3. Collaborating with community agency professionals

4. Working with school staff, family, and community members to advocate for equity, access, and academic success for students

5. Teaching parents and students how to access services in the school and community

6. Involving parents, family, and community members in the delivery of guidance activities and services to students (e.g., career guidance)

7. Using school and student data to advocate for change in the school on behalf of students

8. Helping parents, family, and community members organize support programs for students (e.g., tutoring and mentoring programs)

9. Implementing programs to help family and community members understand the school (e.g., parent and family seminars)

10. Coordinating school-community outreach efforts

11. Providing parent education workshops and seminars

12. Serving on advisory councils or committees in the community

13. Facilitating integration of community services within the school (e.g., mental health and social services housed in the school)

14. Implementing programs to help the school staff understand families and the community (e.g., inservice training on culturally diverse families)

15. Using data to show the benefits of school-family-community partnership programs for students

16. Teaching the staff how to build effective school-family-community partnerships

17. Conducting home visits to families

SOURCE: Adapted from *An Examination of School Counselor Involvement in School-Family-Community Partnerships: Professional School Counseling,* by J. Bryan and C. Holcomb-McCoy.

Resource E

*SOARING Samples
and Worksheets*

SOARING

School Division : Lake School District	School: Roosevelt Middle School	Date: February 2007

Counseling Activity:
Eighth-grade group conferences regarding high school course options, high school scheduling, and diploma requirements.

Standards: Middle School – Career 8: Demonstrate awareness of educational, vocational, and technical training opportunities in high school.	Objectives: At least 50% of eighth-grade students will be able to correctly list all of the high school diploma requirements. 100% of the eighth-grade students will complete registration for high school courses.

Assessment:
Registration forms
Pretest and posttest on high school/diploma requirements

Results:	Impact:
• 435 students completed registration forms—100% • Before group conferences, 58 students out of 435 (13%) could list high school graduation requirements. After group conferences, 398 out of 435 (91%) could list all of the high school graduation requirements Pretest results—13% Posttest results—91%	• 100% of the eighth-grade students completed registration forms for ninth-grade courses. • 78% increase in students' knowledge of the diploma requirements after participating in group conferences. • 8th-grade students' knowledge of requirements for the different diplomas increased from 58 to 398 after completing student group conferences.

8th Grade Students' Knowledge of Graduation Requirements

Network:	Guide:
• Share results with parents in monthly newsletter. • Presentation for faculty and principal. Share information with high school counselors and principals.	• Provide additional information to assist the 37 students. • Coordinate orientation with high school. • Review and revise the lesson.

SOARING

School Division: Virginia			School: Soaring Elementary School			Date: September	
Standards	Objectives	Assessment	Results	Impact		Networking	Guide
EA. 1–Understand the expectations of the educational environment	Kindergarten students will be able to express two expectations after 4 classroom guidance lessons	Pre-, post tests- verbal	20 of 30 students could verbally express at least 2 expectations of school	64% increase in Kindergarten student's knowledge of expectation		Share with parents in monthly newsletter and present to principal and faculty in monthly update	Work with 10 students who were not able to verbalize expectations in a small group or review curriculum

SOURCE: From an unpublished manuscript by Sylinda Gilchrist, PhD, Norfolk State University, Norfolk, VA, 2005. Reprinted with permission from Dr. Sylinda Gilchrist.

SOARING Template

Division

School Division :	School:	Date:

Standard:	Objective:

Assessment:

Results:	Impact:
Network:	Guide:

From an unpublished manuscript by Sylinda Gilchrist, PhD, Norfolk State University, Norfolk, VA, 2005. Reprinted with permission from Dr. Sylinda Gilchrist.

SOARING

Worksheet

Activity: _____

Standards	Objectives	Assessments	Results	Impact	Networking	Guide

From an unpublished manuscript by Sylinda Gilchrist, PhD, Norfolk State University, Norfolk, VA, 2005. Reprinted with permission from Dr. Sylinda Gilchrist.

Suggested Readings by Topic

PREJUDICE, DISCRIMINATION, AND OPPRESSION

Allport, G. W. (1954). *The nature of prejudice.* Garden City, NY: Doubleday.

Boykin, K. (1996). *One more river to cross: Black and gay in America.* New York: Anchor Books.

Fadiman, A. (1998). *The spirit catches you and you fall down.* New York: Farrar, Straus, & Giroux.

Herek, G. M. (1992). Psychological heterosexism and anti-gay violence: The social psychology of bigotry and bashing. In G. M. Herek & K. T. Berrill (Eds.), *Hate crimes: Confronting violence against lesbians and gay men* (pp. 149–169). Newbury Park, CA: Sage Publications.

Kivel, P. (2002). *Uprooting racism: How white people can work for racial justice.* New York: New Society Publishers.

McCall, N. (1994). *Makes me wanna holler: A young black man in America.* New York: Vintage Books.

McIntyre, A. (1997). *Making meaning of whiteness: Exploring racial identity with white teachers.* Albany, NY: State University of New York Press.

Pincus, F. L., & Ehrlich, H. J. (Eds.). (1999). *Race and ethnic conflict: Contending views on prejudice, discrimination, and ethnoviolence.* Boulder, CO: Westview Press.

Plous, S. (Ed.). (2003). *Understanding prejudice and discrimination.* New York: McGraw-Hill.

Razack, S. H. (1998). *Looking white people in the eye: Gender, race, and culture in courtrooms and Classrooms.* Toronto: University of Toronto Press.

Steele, C. M. (1997). A threat in the air: How stereotypes shape intellectual identity and performance. *American Psychologist, 52,* 613–629.

Steinberg, S. (2001). *The ethnic myth: Race, ethnicity, and class in America.* Boston: Beacon Press.

Wells, A. S., & Crain, R. L. (1999). *Stepping over the color line: African-American students in white suburban schools.* New Haven, CT: Yale University Press.

MULTICULTURAL COUNSELING RELATIONSHIPS

Bashur, M. R., Codrington, J. N., & Liang, C. T. H. (2002). Client perspectives of multicultural counseling competence: A qualitative examination. *Counseling Psychologist, 30,* 355–393.

Constantine, M. G. (2002). Predictors of satisfaction with counseling: Racial and ethnic minority clients' attitudes toward counseling and ratings of their counselors' general and multicultural counseling competence. *Journal of Counseling Psychology, 49,* 255–263.

Lee, C. C. (2006). *Multicultural issues in counseling: New approaches to diversity.* Alexandria, VA: American Counseling Association.

McClure, F. H., & Teyber, E. (1996). *Child and adolescent therapy: A multicultural-relational approach.* Orlando, FL: Harcourt Brace College Publishers.

Paniagua, F. (1994). *Assessing and treating culturally diverse clients.* Thousand Oaks, CA: Sage Publications.

Ponterotto, J. G., Casas, J. M., Suzuki, L. A., & Alexander, C. M. (2001). *Handbook of multicultural counseling.* Thousand Oaks, CA: Sage Publications.

Pope-Davis, D. B., Toporek, R. L., Ortega-Villalobos, L., Ligiero, D. P., Liu, W. M., & Russell, J. (1999). Professional and socio-cultural aspects of the counseling relationship. In C. Feltham (Ed.), *Understanding the counseling relationship* (pp. 183–199). Thousand Oaks, CA: Sage Publications.

Schwarzbaum, S. (2004). Low-income latinos and drop out: Strategies to prevent dropout. *Journal of Multicultural Counseling and Development, 32,* 296–306.

Sue, D. W., Ivey, A. E., & Pederson, P. B. (1996). *Theory of multicultural counseling therapy.* Belmont, CA: Wadsworth Publishing.

MIGRATION AND ACCULTURATION

Alba, R., & Nee, V. (2003). *Remaking the American mainstream: Assimilation and contemporary immigration.* Cambridge, MA: Harvard University Press.

Caplan, N., Whitmore, J. K., & Choy, M. H. (1991). *Children of the boat people: A study of educational success.* Ann Arbor, MI: University of Michigan Press.

Lieberson, S., & Waters, M. (1988). *From many strands: Ethnic and racial groups in contemporary America.* New York: Russell Sage Foundation.

Massey, D. S., Durand, J., & Malone, N. (2002). *Beyond smoke and mirrors: Mexican migration in an era of economic integration.* New York: Russell Sage Foundation.

Portes, A., & Rumbaut, R. (1996). *Immigrant America: A portrait* (2nd ed.). Berkeley, CA: University of California Press.

Portes, A., & Rumbaut, R. G. (2001). *Legacies. The story of the immigrant second generation.* Berkeley, CA: University of California Press and Russell Sage Foundation.

Rumbaut, R. G., & Russell Portes, A. (Eds.). (2001). *Ethnicities: Children of immigrants in America.* New York: University of California Press and Sage Foundation.

Suárez-Orozco, C., & Suárez-Orozco, M. M. (2002). *Children of immigration.* Cambridge, MA: Harvard University Press.

Waters, M. C. (1999). *Black identities: West Indian immigrant dreams and American realities.* New York: Russell Sage Foundation.

SOCIAL CLASS

Liu, W. M. (2002). The social class-related experiences of men: Integrating theory and practice. *Professional Psychology: Research and Practice, 33,* 355–360.

Liu, W. M., & Ali, S. R. (2005). Addressing social class in vocational theory and practice: Extending the emancipatory communitarian approach. *The Counseling Psychologist, 33,* 189–196.

Liu, W. M., Ali, S. R., Soleck, G., Hopps, J., Dunston, K., & Pickett, T., Jr. (2004). Using social class in counseling psychology research. *Journal of Counseling Psychology, 51,* 3–18.

Liu, W. M., Soleck, G., Hopps, J., Dunston, K., & Pickett, T. (2004). A new framework to understand social class in counseling: The social class worldview and modern classism theory. *Journal of Multicultural Counseling and Development, 32,* 95–122.

Stern, E. M. (1990). *Psychotherapy and the poverty patient.* Binghamton, NY: Haworth Press.

BILINGUALISM

Biever, J. L., Castano, M. T., Gonzalez, C., Navarro, R. E., Sprowls, C., & Verdinelli, S. (2005). Spanish-language psychotherapy: Therapists' experiences and needs. In S. P. Shohov (Ed.), *Advances in psychology research* (pp. 157–185). Hauppauge, NY: Nova Science Publishers.

Bruhn, R. A., Irby, B. J., Lou, M., Thweatt, W. T., & Lara-Alecio, R. (2005). A model for training bilingual school counselors. In V. Gonzalez & J. Tinajero (Eds.), *Review of research and practice* (pp. 145–161). Mahwah, NJ: Lawrence Erlbaum.

Burck, C. (2004). Living in several languages: Implications for therapy. *Journal of Family Therapy, 26,* 314–339.

Grosjean, F. (1982). *Life with two languages.* Cambridge, MA: Harvard University Press.

Perez-Foster, R. (1998). *The power of language in the clinical process: Assessing and treating the bilingual person.* North Bergen, NJ: Jason Aronson.

Santiago-Rivera, A. L., & Altarriba, J. (2002). The role of language in therapy with the Spanish-English bilingual client. *Professional Psychology: Research and Practice, 33,* 30–38.

ETHNIC OR RACIAL IDENTITY DEVELOPMENT

Gibbs, J., & Hines, A. (1992). Negotiating ethnic identity: Issues for black–white biracial adolescents. In M. Root (Ed.), *Racially mixed people in America* (pp. 223– 238). Newbury Park, CA: Sage Publications.

Helms, J. E. (1993). *Black and white racial identity: Theory, research, and practice.* Westport, CT: Praeger.

Kincheloe, J. J. (1999). The struggle to define and reinvent whiteness: A pedagogical analysis. *College Literature, 26,* 162–194.

Phinney, P., & Rotheram, M. (Eds.). (1987). *Children's ethnic socialization: Pluralism and development.* Thousand Oaks, CA: Sage Publications.

Spencer, M. B., & Markstrom-Adams, C. (1990). Identity processes among racial and ethnic minority children in America. *Child Development, 61,* 290–310.

Tatum, B. D. (1992). Talking about race, learning about racism: The application of racial identity development theory in the classroom. *Harvard Educational Review, 62,* 1–24.

Tatum, B. D. (1997). *Why are all the black kids sitting together in the cafeteria?* New York: Basic Books.

References

Allen, W. R. (2003, October). *And the last shall be first: Racial diversity, distributive justice and affirmative action.* Paper commissioned for the Pullias Lecture Series Center for Higher Education Policy Analysis, Los Angeles, CA.

Allport, G. W. (1954). *The nature of prejudice.* Garden City, NY: Doubleday.

Baca, L. M., & Koss-Chioino, J. D. (1997). Development of a culturally responsive group counseling model for Mexican American adolescents. *Journal of Multicultural Counseling and Development, 25,* 130–141.

Bemak, K. (2000). Transforming the role of the counselor to provide leadership in educational reform through collaboration. *Professional School Counseling, 3,* 323–331.

Bemak, F., & Chung, R. C. (2005). Advocacy as a critical role for urban school counselors: Working toward equity and social justice. *Professional School Counseling, 8,* 196–202.

Bohan-Baker, M., & Little, P. M. D. (2002). *The transition to kindergarten: A review of current research and promising practices to involve families.* Cambridge, MA: Harvard Family Research Project

Boyd-Franklin, N. (1989). *Black families in therapy: A multisystems approach.* New York: Guilford Press.

Brady, D. (2003). Rethinking the sociological measurement of poverty. *Social Forces, 81*(3), 715–752.

Bryan, J. (2005). Fostering resilience and achievement in urban schools through school family-community-partnerships. *Professional School Counseling, 8,* 219–227.

Bryan, J., & Holcomb-McCoy, C. (2004). School counselors' perceptions of their involvement in school family community partnerships. *Professional School Counseling, 7,* 162–171.

Chubb, J. E., & Loveless, T. (2002). *Bridging the achievement gap.* Washington, DC: Brookings Institution Press.

The Civil Rights Project. (2003). Racial disparities in special education: National trends [PowerPoint presentation]. Cambridge, MA: Author. Retrieved January 22, 2007, from www.dpi.state.wi.us/sped/ppt/dis-losen.ppt

Colbert, R. D. (1996). The counselor's role in advancing school and family partnerships. *The School Counselor, 44,* 100–104.

Connell, J. P., Spencer, M. B., & Aber, J. L. (1994). Educational risk and resilience in African-American youth: Context, self, action and outcomes in school. *Child Development, 65,* 493–506.

Denbo, S. J. (2002). Institutional practices that support African American student achievement. In S. J. Denbo & L. M. Beaulieu (Eds.), *Improving schools for African American students* (pp. 55–70). Springfield, IL: Charles C Thomas.

Diller, J. V., & Moule, J. (2004). *Cultural competence.* Belmont, CA: Thomson Wadsworth.

Duncan, C., & Pryzwansky, W. B. (1993). Effects of race, racial identity development, and orientation style on perceived consultant effectiveness. *Journal of Multicultural Counseling and Development, 21,* 88–96.

Education Trust. (2001). *Education in America 2001* [PowerPoint presentation]. Washington DC: Author. Retrieved January 22, 2007, from http://www2.edtrust .org/EdTrust/Product+Catalog/archivesIV.htm

Education Trust. (2006). *Education watch. The nation: Key education facts and figures.* Washington, DC: Author.

Fine, L. (2001). Studies examine racial disparities in special education. *Education Week, 20,* 6.

Fowler, B. (1997). *Pierre Bourdieu and cultural theory; critical investigations.* London: Sage.

Freire, P. (1970). *Pedagogy of the oppressed.* New York: Herder and Herder.

Gandara, P., & Bial, D. (2001). *Paving the way to higher education: K–12 intervention programs for underrepresented youth.* Washington, DC: National Postsecondary Education Cooperative.

Gibbs, J. T. (1985). Can we continue to be color-blind and class-bound? The Counseling Psychologist, 13, 426–435.

Gilchrist, S. (2006). *Counselors are SOARING.* Unpublished manuscript.

Giles, H. C. (2005). Three narratives of parent-educator relationships: Toward counselor repertoires for bridging the urban parent-school divide. *Professional School Counseling, 8*(3), 228–235.

Goldring, L. (2002). The power of school culture. *Leadership, 32,* 32–35.

Gopaul-McNicol, S. A., & Thomas-Presswood, T. (1998). *Working with linguistically and culturally different children: Innovative clinical and educational approaches.* New York: Prentice Hall.

Gottfredson, G., Gottfredson, D. C., Czeh, E. R., Cantor, D., Crosse, S. B., & Hantman, I. (2000). *National study of delinquency prevention in schools.* Ellicott City, MD: Gottfredson Associates. (Final report for the National Institute of Justice, U. S. Department of Justice, Grant # 96-MN-MV-008)

Green, A., & Keys, S. (2001). Expanding the developmental school counseling paradigm: Meeting the needs of the 21st century student. *Professional School Counseling, 5,* 84–95.

Greene, J., & Forster, G. (2003). *Public high school graduation and college readiness rates in the United States.* New York: The Manhattan Institute.

Haskins, R., & Rouse, C. (2005, Spring). Closing achievement gaps [Policy brief]. *The Future of Children* (pp. 1–7). Princeton, NJ: Princeton/Brookings.

Haycock, K. (2001). Closing the achievement gap. *Educational Leadership, 58,* 6–11.

Haycock, K., Jerald, C., & Huang, S. (2001). Closing the gap: Done in a decade. *Thinking K–16, 5,* 3–21.

Helms, J. E. (1990). *Black and White racial identity: Theory, research, and practice.* New York: Greenwood Press.

Henig, J. R., Hula, R. C., Orr, M., & Pedescleaux, D. S. (1999). *The color of school reform: Race, politics, and the challenge of urban education.* Princeton, NJ: Princeton University Press.

Holcomb-McCoy, C. (2004). Assessing the multicultural competence of school counselors: A checklist. *Professional School Counseling, 7,* 178–182.

Holcomb-McCoy, C., & Moore-Thomas, C. (2001). Empowering African American adolescent females. *Professional School Counseling, 5,* 19–25.

Holcomb-McCoy, C., & Myers, J. E. (1999). Multicultural competence and counselor training: A national survey. *Journal of Counseling and Development, 77,* 294–302.

Jackson, J. (2000). What ought psychology do? *American Psychologist, 55,* 328–330.

Johnson, R. (2002). *Using data to close the achievement gap: How to measure equity in our schools.* Thousand Oaks, CA: Corwin Press.

Kalyanpur, M., & Rao, S. S. (1991). Empowering low-income, black families of handicapped children. *American Journal of Orthopsychiatry, 61,* 523–532.

King, M. L., Jr. (1968). The role of the behavioral scientist in the civil rights movement. *Journal of Social Issues, 24,* 1–12.

Kiselica, M., & Robinson, M. (2001). Bringing advocacy counseling to life: The history, issues, and human dramas of social justice work in counseling. *Journal of Counseling and Development, 79,* 387–397.

Lee, C. C. (1995). *Counseling for diversity: A guide for school counselors and related professionals.* Boston: Allyn and Bacon.

Lee, C. (2005). *Multicultural issues in counseling.* Alexandria, VA: American Counseling Association.

Lee, C., & Richardson, B. L. (1991). *Multicultural issues in counseling: New approaches to diversity.* Alexandria, VA: American Association for Counseling and Development.

Liu, W. M., & Ali, S. R. (2005). Addressing social class and classism in vocational theory and practice. *The Counseling Psychologist, 33,* 189–196.

Locke, D. C. (1998). *Increasing multicultural understanding: A comprehensive model.* Thousand Oaks, CA: Sage.

Losen, D., & Orfield, G. (2002). *Racial inequity in special education.* Cambridge, MA: Harvard Education Publishing Group.

Manset, G., St. John, E. P., Simmons, A., Gordon, D., Musoba, G. D., & Klingerman, K. (2000). *Wisconsin's high performing/high poverty schools.* Naperville, IL: North Central Regional Laboratory.

Marshall, P. L. (2002). Racial identity and challenges of educating white youths for cultural diversity. *Multicultural Perspectives, 4*(3), 9–14.

National Assessment of Educational Progress. (2004). *NAEP 2004 Trends in academic progress.* Washington, DC: U.S. Department of Education, National Center for Education Statistics.

National Center for Education Statistics. (2006). *The Condition of education 2006.* Washington DC: U.S. Department of Education. (NCES 2006-071)

Noam, G. G. (1999). The psychology of belonging: Reformulating adolescent development. In A. H. Esman (Ed.), *Adolescent psychiatry: Development and clinical studies* (pp. 49–68). Hillsdale, NJ: The Analytic Press.

Norris, D. M., & Spurlock, J. (1992). Racial and cultural issues impacting on countertransference. In J. R. Brandell (Ed.), *Countertransference in psychotherapy with children and adolescents* (pp. 91–123). Northvale, NJ: Aronson.

Ogbu, J. (1994). Racial stratification and education in the United States: Why inequality persists. *Teachers College Record, 96,* 264–298.

Oswald, D. P., Coutinho, M. J., Best, A. M., & Singh, N. N. (1999). Ethnic representation in special education: The influence of school-related income and demographic variables. *Journal of Special Education, 32,* 194–206.

Phinney, J. S. (1990). Ethnic identity in adolescents and adults: Review of research. *Psychological Bulletin, 108,* 499–514.

Ponterotto, J., & Casas, H. (1987). In search of multicultural competence within counselor education programs. *Journal of Counseling and Development, 65,* 430–434.

Pope-Davis, D. B., Reynolds, A. L., Dings, J. G., & Ottavi, T. M. (1994). Multicultural competencies of doctoral interns at university counseling centers: An exploratory investigation. *Professional Psychology: Research and Practice, 25,* 466–470.

Prilleltensky, I. (1994). *The morals and politics of psychology: Psychological discourse and the status quo.* Albany, NY: State University of New York Press.

Proweller, A. (1999). Shifting identities in private education: Reconstructing race at/in the cultural center. *Teachers College Record, 100,* 776–808.

Slavin, R. (2002). Evidence-based education policies: Transforming educational practice and research. *Educational Researcher, 31*(7), 15–21.

Slavin, R. E., Madden, N. A., Dolan, L. J., Wasik, B. A., Ross, S. M., Smith, L. J., & Dianda, M. (1998). Success for all: Achievement outcomes of a schoolwide reform model. In J. Crane (Ed.), *Social programs that work* (pp. 43–74). New York: Russell Sage Foundation.

Steele, C. M. (1997). A threat in the air: How stereotypes shape intellectual identity and performance. *American Psychologist, 52,* 613–629.

Stone, C. B., & Dahir, C. A. (2004). *School counselor accountability: A measure of student success.* New York: Prentice Hall.

Sue, D. W., Arredondo, P., & McDavis, R. (1992). Multicultural counseling competencies and standards: A call to the profession. *Journal of Counseling and Development, 70,* 477–486.

Teachers College Columbia University. (2004). *A campaign for equity: 2004 Annual Report.* New York: Author.

Terrell Y. L., & Cheatham, H. E. (1996). Creating a therapeutic alliance: A multicultural perspective. In J. L. DeLucia-Waack (Ed.), *Multicultural counseling competencies: Implications for training and practice* (pp. 63–88). Alexandria, VA: Association for Counselor Education and Supervision.

Toporek, R. L., & Liu, W. M. (2001). Advocacy in Counseling: Addressing issues of race, class, and gender oppression. In D. B. Pope-Davis & H. L. K. Coleman (Eds.), *The intersection of race, class, and gender in counseling psychology* (pp. 385–416). Thousand Oaks, CA: Sage Publications.

Ungar, M. (2006). *Strengths-based counseling with at-risk youth.* Thousand Oaks, CA: Corwin Press.

U.S. Department of Education. (2000). *National Center for Educational Statistics, Digest of Education Statistics.* Washington, DC: Author.

U.S. Department of Education. (2004). *To assure the free appropriate public education of all children with disabilities: Twenty-fourth annual report to Congress on the implementation of the Individuals with Disabilities Education Act.* Washington, DC: Author.

U.S. Department of Education. (2006). *NCES, parent and family involvement in education survey, 2002–2003.* Washington, DC: Author.

U.S. Department of Education, National Center for Education Statistics. (2006). *The condition of education 2006*. Washington, DC: U.S. Government Printing Office. (NCES 2006-071)

Wong, Y. J. (2006). Strength-centered therapy: A social constructionist, virtues-based psychotherapy. *Psychotherapy: Theory, Research, Practice, Training, 43,* 133–146.

Zayas, L. H. (2001). Incorporating struggles with racism and ethnic identity in therapy with adolescents. *Clinical Social Work Journal, 29,* 361–373.

Zeichner, K. M. (2003). The adequacies and inadequacies of three current strategies to recruit, prepare, and retain the best teachers for all students. *Teachers College Record, 105*(3), 490–519.

Zins, J. E., & Erchul, W. P. (2002). Best practices in school consultation. In A. Thomas & J. Grimes (Eds.), *Best practices in school psychology—IV* (pp. 625–643). Washington, DC: National Association of School Psychologists.

Zutlevics, T. L. (2002). Towards a theory of oppression. *Ratio, 15,* 80–102.

Index

Note: In page references, f indicates figures, e indicates exercises and t indicates tables.

preschool programs and, 11
school culture and, 63
SFC partnerships and, 79
special education and, 9
standardized tests and, 7
See also Hispanics; Students-of-color
Leadership:
achievement gap and, 13, 14, 120
assessing equity and, 124, 125
bias and, 102
counseling and, 130
data and, 83
school culture and, 64, 133
SFC partnerships and, 69–70, 72, 73
Leadership teams, 69, 123–125
Learning disabilities, 9
See also Disabilities
Lee, C., 17, 18
Legislators, 72
See also Politics
Levine, A., 20
Little, P. M. D., 25
Liu, W. M., 40
Locke, D. C., 60
Losen, D., 9, 110
Loveless, T., 6
Low-achieving students, 24–25, 106
Low-income, 33–34
achievement gap and, 3, 5–6
assessing equity and, 123, 124
coordinating student services
and, 27–28
counseling and, 39, 115
gatekeeping and, 107
gifted programs and, 111–112
less-experienced teachers and, 8
preschool programs and, 11
school readiness and, 10–11
SFC partnerships and, 72, 79
test scores and, 25
See also Poverty

Manset, G., 13
Marginalizing students, 23, 39,
45–46, 102, 114
Marshall, P. L., 20, 45
Master schedules, 64, 105–107, 132
Mathematics, 1, 2, 10, 116, 125
McDavis, R., 18, 46
Mental health issues, 18, 49
Mental retardation, 8–9, 110

Mexican Americans. *See* Hispanics;
Latinos
Middle-to-high income, 3, 6, 11
See also Low-income
Migration. *See* Immigrants
Minorities:
counseling and, 115, 126, 129, 130
ethnic identity and, 42
peer pressure and, 13
White racial superiority
and, 45–46
See also Students-of-color
Mission statements, 68, 69, 72
Moore-Thomas, C., 42
Motor development, 50
Moule, J., 24
Multicultural counseling,
18, 46–47, 126–131
Multiculturalism, 17
Myers, J. E., 46
Myths, viii, 63, 96

National Assessment of
Educational Progress, 7, 8
National Educational Longitudinal
Study (NELS), 111
National Model, 4–5, 4(f), 14, 82
National Standards. *See* Standards
Native Americans:
achievement gap and, 6
assessing equity and, 123
college education and, 9–10
intervention planning/culture
and, 51
school culture and, 63
special education and, 8–9, 110
See also Students-of-color
No Child Left Behind Act, 82
Noam, G. G., 42
Norris, D. M., 33
North Central Regional Education
Laboratory (NCREL), 13
Nutrition, 12, 63, 64

Ogbu, J., 13
Oppression, 19–20, 31–32
assessing equity and, 124
bias and, 27, 95–102, 98–99, 100
counseling and, 17, 39, 114
discomfort/fear and, 33
social justice and, 18